The Power of
Positive
Handwriting

Elayne V. Lindberg
with
Gary Lindberg

Wisdom
Editions
Minneapolis

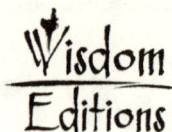

Wisdom Editions

Minneapolis

FOURTH EDITION DECEMBER 2022

10 9 8 7 6 5 4

ISBN: 978-1-960250-27-8

Dedicated with love to Elayne's grandson and Gary's son,
Brendan Lindberg, 1972 - 2016

The Power of
Positive
Handwriting

Elayne V. Lindberg
with
Gary Lindberg

TABLE OF CONTENTS

PART I

PART II

PART III

INTRODUCTION

While earning my Bachelor of Arts degree in psychology from the University of Minnesota, no mention was ever made of handwriting analysis in any of my classes. I celebrated my new degree in Las Vegas and, just for fun, a good friend and I had our handwriting analyzed at the Circus Circus casino. The graphologist, working chiefly for entertainment value, glanced at my writing and said I would make a good psychologist. My companion, a defensive linebacker for the Denver Broncos, was told he had an abundance of literary ability. The graphologist revealed other personality traits that were extremely accurate and made it seem like she was psychic, though she explained that graphology was a legitimate science and she had previously worked for a judge as a handwriting analyst. I was immediately hooked.

Everything the graphologist explained to us became a reality. With her validation, perhaps, I became a clinical psychologist and my friend, Jim Sullivan, quit professional football, moved from Denver to Los Angeles and became a screenwriter.

Elayne Lindberg, the primary author of this book, also chanced upon handwriting analysis while seeking a new path after being a homemaker for twenty years. She had no interest in the more conventional opportunities until she attended a lecture on handwriting analysis and was instantly captivated. She investigated several different methods of education and, like me, chose Graphoanalysis™ because their analytical methods had been carefully standardized. Elayne became a Master Graphoanalysis (MGA) but recognized early in her career that other methods of study could also be useful.

Elayne titled her book *The Power of Positive Handwriting*. After studying and working in the field for over forty years, I agree that the knowledge graphologists possess should be used to achieve positive results for individuals, to encourage and guide them into leading a more positive and fulfilling life.

While performing assessments in the neuropsychological department of a hospital, performing contract personnel selection and team building for corporations, and working as a clinical psychologist, I have come to believe that in many cases handwriting analysis is the most efficient and effective way to help the client. It is fast (speed can be essential when a client is suicidal). It can be done without permission (courts have called it "behavior in public," like a smile or tears, which can be freely observed and analyzed.) And it is a very inexpensive therapeutic choice for personal insights.

To my knowledge, Elayne was the first handwriting analyst to use "graphotherapy" as a means of helping individuals holistically change their personalities, and thus their lives, by making positive changes in their handwriting. Although individual traits are considered in this book, Elayne teaches the reader how to evaluate the predominant, most global factors in handwriting such as slant, pressure, size, form of letters and connections of letters, all of which need to be considered rather than just taking a single-trait approach. Every trait in our writing has a right to be there but can be modified and rebalanced

As an experienced clinical psychologist, I have taught a Minnesota State Board-approved class on graphology to psychologists, social workers, teachers and even nurses. The class taught these professionals how to incorporate handwriting analysis into their own practices. In my professional life I most often work with people who have social anxiety disorder or "fear of people." Isolation, and the accompanying depression that can follow, sometimes leads people to thoughts of suicide. When I meet with a new client, I ask them to write out answers to specific questions to make sure they're not having this problem. If they are, I explain that if they do not like the life they're leading they can change it. In these cases, the conversation often turns to graphotherapy.

Of course, if a client has a plan for suicide and a determined plan to complete it, immediate interventions are called for such as creating a suicide pact in which the client agrees not to attempt suicide before contacting the therapist or other agencies. In some cases, the client may choose to enter a more highly structured program to ensure safety. needs to be committed to a hospital or an outpatient setting to ensure safety.

I have seen remarkable results from graphotherapy. After three months of graphotherapy and counseling, a teenage girl who continued to say she "wanted to leave"—meaning *leave this earth*—turned herself outward instead of inward. From being terrified of everything and everyone, she developed the self-confidence to deliver an oral report to a class and went on to sing a solo in front of a large audience. She learned to identify others who were afraid like she had been and found the strength to help them.

In another case, a highly intelligent young man who couldn't finish high school because of an intense fear of leaving home quickly completed his GED after graphotherapy and counseling. He became a manager at a major retailer and was able to make formal presentations to his fifty direct reports. He has made plans to attend college.

A final example is a young woman who could also not leave the home she shared with her mother because of her countless fears. She is now a corporate attorney. Her now busy (rather than barren) life includes being a wife and mother.

So, read this book by Elayne Lindberg knowing that a positive change is in store. It is my opinion as a graphologist and experienced clinical psychologist that people are not really afraid of success as some propose. I believe that people thrive on it. And once a "success personality" is formed—which can happen if you follow the instructions in this book—doors can open wide whether the success you desire is financial, material, social or spiritual.

Jane Hollis
Psychologist Emeritus, MGA

PART I

THE BEGINNING OF AN ADVENTURE

At one time I had a long list of *If Only's* in my life. I freely had made the decision to stay home with my children during their developing years; I knew that mothering was one of the world's most rewarding experiences. But what mother at one time or another hasn't said to herself, "If only I were free from all this?"

And then one day I was.

When the children were finally gone, my dissatisfaction with myself reached an all-time peak. All those years invested in mothering. I was a darn good mother, too... but that was the problem. I was a professional mom with no kids. What I needed was a job — no, a *career!*

Scared to death, with all my *If Only's* screaming at me, I started making the rounds. And it was worse than I thought it was going to be. Over and over I was told that I was completely, totally unqualified for anything whatsoever. My long list of *If Only's* grew even longer with each job interview.

When I was finally hired, no one was more surprised than me. My self-esteem had bottomed out. So here I was, Elayne Lindberg, Ph.D in Motherhood, working as a busgirl in a cafeteria. Was this the lowest I could sink? No. Two months later I was fired for not properly cleaning the salt and pepper shakers. There is only one good thing about unemployment: you have plenty of time to think. I used this time to great advantage; I wallowed in self-pity and mused about my many inadequacies.

One night a good friend pried me loose from my doldrums and dragged me into a lecture on handwriting analysis. The "graphotherapist" promised that after the lecture she would give a short, personal (but public) analysis of each person who attended. The prospect of this roomful of strangers being told the murky secrets of my personality made me try to disappear into my chair. But I couldn't.

Each of us in the audience was asked to write a short note on pre-numbered cards. These scrawlings were then collected and Josephine Nash began to speak. She was fascinating! But her claims seemed too fantastic to be true. A person's handwriting, she told us, could reveal to the trained eye an amazing amount about that person's personality. Each stroke spoke volumes. The slant of each letter and the heaviness of the pen uncovered secrets.

The lecture finished, Josephine plunged into the first of her "instant analyses." She looked at one of the cards, studied it for a moment and then her eyes brightened. "This person is persistent, has good determination and exceptional mental qualities," she said.

I looked around the room, wondering who this person might be. I settled on two candidates.

"Oh, this is card number 12, by the way," Josephine said. "So you know who you are."

Card 12. Card 12! That was me! Either she had read the number wrong or this handwriting stuff was sheer bogus. That didn't describe me at all.

"You have all the necessary qualities to succeed," Josephine continued, "but you haven't succeeded yet. The personality trait that is holding you back the most is your sensitivity. You do not hear what is positive about yourself because of past and imagined hurts. This prevents you from ever looking at yourself objectively."

And suddenly I knew she was right. She had predicted that I wouldn't even recognize a description of my own personality. As she continued, I realized that Mrs. Nash was offering me hope. On a blackboard she showed the handwriting stroke that indicated hyper-sensitivity... and showed how to alter it. By changing the stroke, she said, the undesirable trait itself could be changed. All that was required was awareness and diligent practice.

When I left the lecture hall that night I knew what I had to do. I began practicing the altered strokes faithfully. At first it was difficult, but little by little I began to feel at home with the changes. And I began to see myself more clearly, more objectively! I noticed, however, that whenever I started to feel sorry for myself, the old stroke started to creep into my handwriting.

My life was changing! In one evening I had found another direction for my life.

All this took place many years ago. Today, after twenty years of research and study, I am a Master Graphoanalyst myself. That night in the lecture hall I began a new, exciting journey in life that has taken me on adventure I never could have dreamed of. This book is my way of sharing that adventure with you. I hope that what I have learned will touch you, excite you, and give you the same hope it has given me.

WHAT I HAVE LEARNED

The field of handwriting analysis, like all fields of science and technology, is full of special terms and jargon. To begin with, there are several different names for the study and analysis of handwriting.

Graphology is a general term for all forms and systems of handwriting analysis that have as a goal the understanding of personality and character. Taken from the greek "grapho"—meaning I write and "logos"—meaning method or concept.

Graphoanalysis is a copyrighted, trade-marked name for a certain school of specialized training in handwriting analysis. The aim of this training is to determine character and personality traits of a writer from handwriting samples.

Graphology, Graphoanalysis, Grapho-Therapy, and ***Graphotypes;*** are all forms of handwriting analysis. No matter what the specific school, the discipline is similar. Each branch of the basic science is a system which produces scientifically validated data. Graphoanalysts operated under a strict code of ethics as well.

Handwriting analysis can give a surprisingly accurate picture of a personality. Its use can provide a knowledgeable analyst many clues to a writer's emotional response pattern and thinking process.

I am an MGA, a Master Graphoanalyst. As with most professions there is a prescribed course in obtaining the necessary training. I chose the curriculum at the International Graphoanalysis School. A student can expect to spend three to four years to complete the coursework needed for an MGA.

Many people think that handwriting analysis is little more than fortune telling. This misconception is compounded when a shopper at the local bookstore must search through the *Occult* section to find books on graphology. Actually, handwriting analysis is a proven science. There has been extensive depth-research to determine the correlation of individual handwriting strokes to personality traits. Every stroke has a specific meaning. The study of handwriting began in Italy in the 17th Century. In the three and one-half centuries of research since, we have learned a great deal about connection between handwriting and the brain behind it.

THE HISTORY OF HANDWRITING ANALYSIS

Ever since writing was first used for communication, people have understood intuitively that the way we write reveals something about us. Thinking people throughout history have remarked on the changes that stress, age and illness impose on handwriting. Look at your signature on that mortgage! Grandpa's last letter doesn't look much like his first love letter. And many years ago, John Quincy Adams' trembling handwriting betrayed his fatal illness.

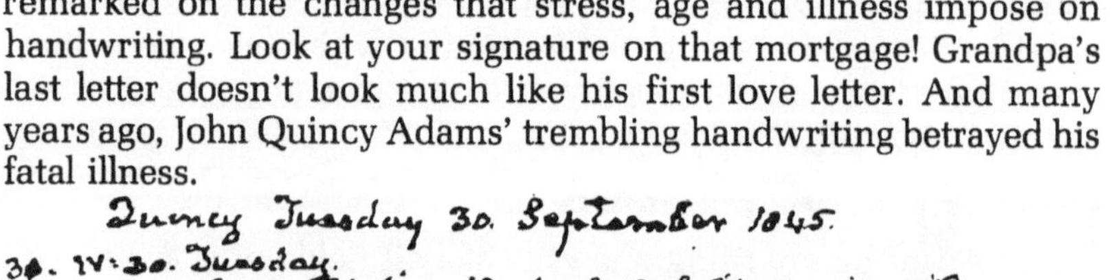
Quincy Tuesday 30. September 1845.
30. IV. 30. Tuesday.
From this time the total disability to write with my own hand compels me to discontinue the daily journal of my life.
I took the Pills prescribed by Dr. Woodward last evening, before going to

Fig. 1: Notice Adam's trembling strokes. An aide had to finish this passage for him.

The Ancient Romans may have been amateur handwriting analysts. Suetonius; once said of a poet to Emperor Augustus, "I notice most this in his writing: he does not separate his words and he does not carry over the extra letters at the end of his verses, but he places them beneath the line and circles them." Suetonius never explained what these observations meant to him, but he seemed to take for granted that the way a person wrote told something about the way that person thought.

In the Orient, the Chinese noted the relationship between handwriting and personality as early as the 11th Century. But it was not until the Seventeenth Century that handwriting analysis was seriously considered as a technique to uncover character traits. An Italian Camillo Baldi published in 1622 a treatise called "How to Understand the Habits and Qualities of the Writer from His Written Letters."

Baldi wrote, "It is obvious that all persons write in their own way... These... traits of character can be recognized in any handwriting... Yet it is necessary to observe carefully whether the characteristics of handwriting recur, moreover whether they are in any way artificial..." Baldi, a Professor of Medicine, Philosophy and Logic, became famous in his time. Using his book, his followers blithely went from castle to castle analyzing the handwriting of lords and ladies. Baldi's ideas spread throughout Europe and even Louis XIV, King of France, had his handwriting analyzed.

In the Eighteenth Century, the Swiss philosopher Lavater became interested in handwriting analysis. He collected many handwriting samples and made some good guesses about their meaning.

In the Nineteenth Century a sort of school of amateur graphology arose in France. It was the Frenchman Abbe Jean-Hippolyte Michon who coined the word "graphology" and published the first description of a system for studying handwriting. The zealous Michon even published a special interest magazine, "La Graphologie," and founded the Graphological Society of Paris.

Michon's early method was simple but effective. In his own words: "We gathered together a series of writings presenting an identical stroke, and we tried to find in the individuals the corresponding character trait. Also, given ten people of similar temperament, we searched their writings for the graphological sign." Michon was the first to perform actual research in the field of handwriting analysis and as a pioneer was bound to make some mistakes. He deduced, for example, that the absence of a stroke in the handwriting meant that the writer possessed the opposite trait. If a writer had failed to exhibit the stroke that indicates greed or avarice, Michon would have assigned that writer a generous nature. This has been proven to be a dangerous mistake!

During this Nineteenth Century many great minds latched onto the concept of handwriting analysis. Robert Browning and his wife, Elizabeth Barrett Browning, were fascinated by it. She wrote:

Dark words on white paper
Betray the soul.

Edgar Allen Poe analyzed handwriting and published his analysis in the *Southern Literary Messenger*. It is not clear whether he was familiar with all the current European thought (instead of "graphology" he called his process "autography"), but it was clear that he was on the right track. He may have made mistakes, but instinctively he understood the basic process.

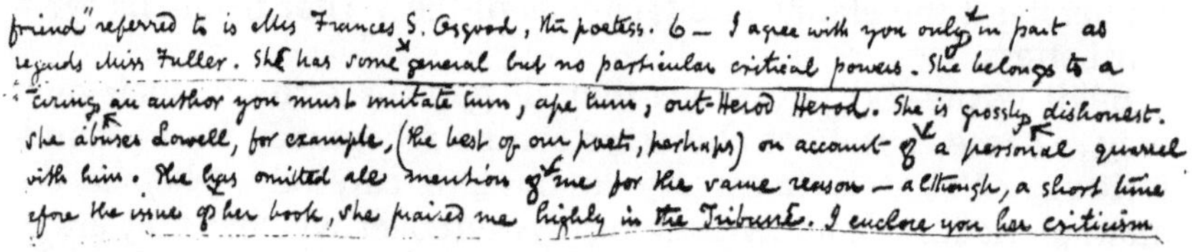
friend" referred to is Mrs Frances S. Osgood, the poetess. 6 — I agree with you only in part as
regards Miss Fuller. She has some general but no particular critical powers. She belongs to a
criticizing an author you must imitate him, ape him, out-Herod Herod. She is grossly dishonest.
She abuses Lowell, for example, (the best of our poets, perhaps) on account of a personal quarrel
with him. She has omitted all mention of me for the same reason — although, a short time
before the issue of her book, she praised me highly in the Tribune. I enclose you her criticism

Fig.2: Edgar Allen Poe's handwriting. Notice the figure "8's" in his writing, a sign of literary ability.

Errors aside, Michon, Poe and their contemporaries usually based their interpretations on observation and common sense. A lot of research since has validated many of the conclusions of this common sense approach. **As you learn the fundamentals of handwriting analysis you will gain a greater appreciation for how logical and simple the basic concepts are.**

During the Nineteenth Century, however, not all graphologists were scrupulous in method. Serious scientists began to view graphology as folk science to be taken with a grain of salt. The discipline was in great need of finding some.

At last a respected psychologist named Alfred Binet, who had invented the I.Q. Test, began to work with graphologists to develop research of the subject into a scientific form. In the early course of his investigations, Binet tested seven graphologists by asking them to distinguish between the handwriting of 37 highly successful, intelligent men and the handwriting of 37 less successful men of average intelligence. All of the graphologists did better than chance and one was amazingly 92% correct! The study was one of the first scientific tests of the validity of handwriting analysis.

In an attempt to determine whether interpretation by graphologists was better than mere guesses, another researcher, O. Bobertag, devised an interesting study. Six graphologists each were given the same five handwriting samples and asked to write personality sketches based on the writing. The 30 sketches were then given to 15 friends of each handwriting subject for evaluation. About 85% of the traits assigned to the subjects were judged to be accurate by those who knew the subjects best. Based on these and other studies, research into graphology exploded over the next hundred years.

During the Twentieth Century new investigators from many different disciplines entered the field. Nobel Prize-winner Henri Bergson made many research contributions. Swiss psychologist Max Pulver discovered the importance of "unconscious drives" in handwriting. Other investigators emphasized Freudian or Jungian psychology and some focused on symbolic communication. The Strang Clinic in New York City studied the use of handwriting analysis to diagnose cancer and heart disease. The New School for Social Research in New York teaches graphology as a medical diagnostic tool.

Today the science of handwriting analysis continues to expand and improve with each new wave of information. Computers and other electronic devices are being used to analyze data from handwriting samples. Progress in understanding is inevitable. And yet the flow of research continues to validate the basic reliability of handwriting analysis to identify personality traits and distinguish individual writers from each other.

BRAINWRITING

In 1939, the American psychologist Lawrence K. Frank first spoke of "projective methods" of personality study. "Projection" is described as the behavior that brings to the exterior the basic tendencies of a personality. Projections, in other words, are *outward expressions of inner events*. We all project ourselves. We "express ourselves" when we speak, when we act, and when we react to any stimulus.

When using projective methods of investigation, a scientist provides carefully selected ways for a subject to express himself. Examples include the "word association" techniques used by Jung, the spots and splotches used by Rorschach, and the so-called "Thematic Apperception" tests. These various methods each encourage a subject to express himself or herself. The results give the psychologist insights into the subject's personality.

Graphoanalysis is another excellent investigative method; handwriting is another way we express ourselves. It is a gesture that originates not in the hand, but in the brain. When we write, we are aided by visual perceptions (taking place in the occipital lobe) and auditory perceptions (taking place in the temporal lobe.) To put it another way, we write words that have been "heard" or "read."

The messages that control the handling of the writing instrument come from the parietal lobe, the psycho-sensory area of the brain. When we learn as children to write, it seems to require great effort because writing at this early stage is mostly a conscious and voluntary act. Each movement of the hand springs from the motor and psychomotor area of the cerebral cortex. The nerve impulses are then sent to the hand and fingers. Once we have become adept at writing, the motor impulses that guide our hands no longer come from the cortex; they come instead from the more primitive thalamus and globus pallidus, the instinctive portions of the brain.

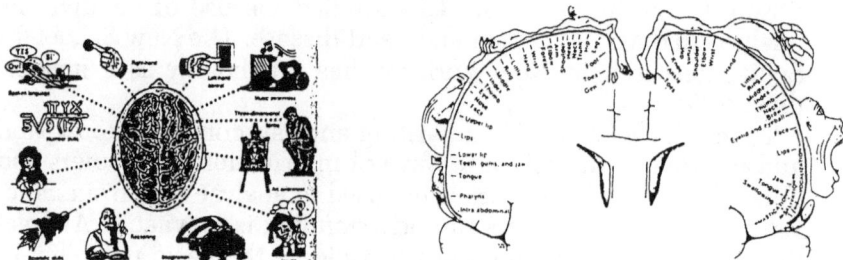

Penfield's operating room "experiments" also made possible the construction of a *motor homunculus, literally a cartoon of the body surface drawn to scale and representing body parts aligned not according to their actual size but rather to the extent to which they are involved in skilled movements.*

Fig. 3: *The human brain controls handwriting.*

A common medical procedure for determining brain damage is called an EEG (electroencephalogram.) The test is conducted by attaching electrodes to the subject's scalp, through which brain waves are sensed and conducted to a machine. This machine converts the brain waves onto chart paper resulting in lines that contain many jagged peaks and valleys. A trained neurologist can "read" this writing and accurately interpret what is going on in the subject's brain.

Because handwriting is so directly controlled by the brain, it can be compared to the charts produced by an EEG. Brain waves, of course, provide an entirely different kind of information, but within the highly individual handwriting strokes of each writer is a subtle but revealing personal message communicated directly by the brain. A trained graphoanalyst can "read" this message and accurately interpret the personality traits it expresses. And it requires no sophisticated machine, unless you consider the human organism.

DIFFERENT STROKES FOR DIFFERENT FOLKS

Handwriting is the most common permanent record of the personalities and inner lives of people everywhere. No wonder handwriting analysis has become so widely used. Handwriting fixes in time and space the inner workings of human minds, freezing it for us to examine. Perhaps that's why the poet marveled:

"Whence did the wondrous mystic art arise
Of printing speech and speaking to the eyes:
That by tracing magic lines,
Are taught how to embody and to color thought!"

Children begin to use symbols for self-expression early in life. Often they learn to scribble before they learn to speak. Even primitive peoples without written languages use symbols for self-expression. Can such "scrawlings" also be analyzed? Yes, they can.

The Chinese use a written language that is based on pictographs. Pictographs are a kind of "picture" of objects or events that have evolved over the centuries from representational drawings to very stylized, bare-bones symbols.

Original character	Simplified character	Pīnyīn	Meaning
國 (11)	国 (7)	guó	country, nation
廠 (15)	厂 (2)	chǎng	factory
門 (7)	门 (3)	mén	door
會 (13)	会 (6)	huì	meeting, can
馬 (10)	马 (3)	mǎ	horse
幾 (11)	几 (2)	jǐ	several

*The number in parentheses indicates the number of strokes.

Fig 4: Each Chinese character has developed from a more representational drawing.

Over time, the Chinese, Sumerians and ancient Egyptians added another twist in symbolic expressions: "ideographs." Each of these figures was an arbitrary symbol that represented an abstract idea.

There came a time, though, when primitive cultures found a need to express themselves still more adequately through writing. The Phoenicians are a good example. They were a culture that revolved around the trading of goods in the Mediterranean. Because of this active commerce, there was a need for accurate bookkeeping and long distance communications with other cultures. Out of this need grew a solution, the creation of a simpler method of writing that used a symbol to represent each spoken sound. The term "phonetic" comes from "Phoenician."

The Phoenicians' system was indeed a revolutionary change. It greatly simplified record keeping; accountants could now add a brand new item to their ledgers without inventing a new symbol to represent it. Before the phonetic alphabet, every new word required a writer to invent a symbol for it and communicate its meaning to everyone who would have to interpret it.

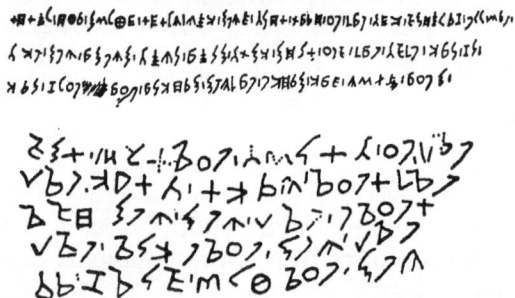

Fig. 5: *The Phoenicians; invention of the alphabet enabled an early civilization to thrive.*

The Greeks further developed the Phoenician invention into an alphabet that enabled a great culture to flourish in a more primitive time. The Greek alphabet helped spread Greek ideas and culture throughout the early Old World. The Romans then borrowed much from the Greek culture and the Roman Empire took its turn at expansion, caused as much by the written word as by the sword.

The Greek alphabet, the Roman alphabet and other symbolic systems provide us with records of centuries of human life and achievement. Without writing, history is impossible to record. And yet the written word can tell us more than the content of the message communicated. It can tell us much about the communicator. Despite the system, style of writing, culture or language, handwriting of any age can be analyzed by a trained graphoanalyst. This is possible because the graphoanalyst ignores the words and recognizes that even the individual letters are not an adequate basis for analysis. The graphoanalysis focuses on the element that all writings have in common: **strokes.**

HANDWRITING AND GRAPHOANALYSIS

Milton Bunker must get the credit for discovering the importance of the handwriting stroke. His methodical research over many years finally validated many conclusions and introduced a critical focus to the otherwise haphazard field of graphology. Bunker's theories were supported by the analysis of tens of thousands of handwriting samples. From these samples he discovered that over 100 personality traits could be clearly identified in handwriting.

Milton Bunker eventually coined the word "graphoanalysis" for his system and founded The International Graphoanalysis Society and affiliated school in Chicago, Illinois. **We owe Mr. Bunker a great debt for his extensive research and the discovery of a basic principle that is perhaps the most exciting of all: *graphotherapy!***

Bunker's research and experimentation showed that deliberate and conscious change of a meaningful handwriting stroke could alter the corresponding personality trait in the writer. This means that a **simple handwriting modification can result in *profound personality changes for the better!***

After fifteen years of my own research, I am more convinced than ever that Bunker was right. And I'm convinced also of the unlimited potential for improvement that exists in the tools he has given us.

Today, throughout the world, graphoanalysis is being used by educated, informed people to fulfill a host of objectives. New applications continue to be found, but here are the most common uses of handwriting analysis.

VOCATIONAL ANALYSIS

As an aid to vocational analysis, handwriting has been utilized since 1812. Vocational analysis is widely accepted throughout Europe today. It is reported that 85% of all European businesses use some form of graphology for personnel selection and management screening. In America the technique has been accepted more slowly, but even here about 5000 companies hire the services of professional handwriting analysts every year.

While Europeans favor handwriting analysis, Americans seem to favor machines such as the "lie detector" (or polygraph.) Court battles, however, have been convincing many employers to find alternate screening aids. The polygraph has been shown to be fallible and many individuals have brought invasion of privacy suits against employers who impose polygraph tests upon them. Twenty-six states currently have laws restricting the use of polygraph tests and similar legislation has been proposed in seventeen more.

Clearly, the polygraph is less than perfect. Dr. David Lykken of the University of Minnesota has researched and written extensively on the use of the machine. He claims the same degree of accuracy could be achieved by flipping a coin. Even when accurate results are obtained, the polygraph reveals only past behavior. It cannot reveal the deeper inate personal characteristics that are so useful in personnel screening and hiring.

The courts are at the forefront of the battle to protect us from the polygraph invasion of privacy, yet at the same time Supreme Court decisions seem to encourage the use of handwriting analysis. The Fifth Amendment guarantees all of us that we will not be required to witness against ourselves in a court of law, but handwriting is legally considered to be a "physical characteristic." The Court put it this way: "handwriting, like speech, is repeatedly shown to the public, and there is no more expectation of privacy in the physical characteristics of a person's script than there is in the tone of his voice." Since handwriting is considered public behavior there can be no intrusion of privacy through analysis.

More and more personnel directors in America are following their European counterparts in accepting handwriting analysis because it has been shown to be a valuable tool in personnel screening. Hundreds of personality traits can be evaluated to determine the job applicant's integrity, persistence, job satisfaction, self-confidence and many other other factors.

Large corporations often use my services in hiring. When a company must choose between several people for a specific job, I analyze the handwriting of the candidates to help determine the best match of applicant and job. Even when the candidates have similar resumes, handwriting analysis can help identify the differing personal characteristics that may be important. For example, in judging candidates for a **secretarial position,** aside from previous professional training and experience I would look for an applicant who:

1. Pays close attention to detail.
2. Has good comprehension and readily understands what other people are trying to communicate.
3. Is diplomatic.
4. Has good manual dexterity.
5. Has good organizational ability.
6. Shows versatility.

Later in this book you will learn how to identify a variety of personal characteristics such as these through handwriting analysis. Once the basics have been learned, a whole new world of discovery and understanding is open to you. The same principals, in fact, apply around the world. There are many languages and styles of writing, but whether the writer communicates in English or Swahili, handwriting analysis can reveal the writer's innermost personality traits.

In Japan last year I visited with a respected Japanese graphonalyst. I analyzed his Japanese writing and he analyzed my scrawlings in English. We were able to to this because handwriting analysis does not focus on the meaning of words, but on individual strokes. The secrets of personality unlocked by an individual stroke of the pen is not changed by language.

If you accept this premise, you may feel a bit ill at ease knowing that a graphoanalyst can know you so intimately from your handwriting. Well, relax. **Handwriting analysis is a science of understanding. Handwriting not only reveals our faults and negative traits, but our strengths of character as well. We can change many of our negatives once we identify them (which is what this book is about), and we can be encouraged by our positives. Getting to know ourselves better through handwriting — and discovering methods of improvement — is the quest that is just beginning.**

PSYCHIATRIC USES OF HANDWRITING ANALYSIS

Handwriting analysis is often used to help phychiatrists in their work. I work with a leading Minneapolis psychiatrist who deals with severely withdrawn people. His patients are so depressed they are often not able to talk about their problems. That condition makes talk therapy difficult, but with handwriting analysis it is not impossible. Handwriting analysis helps open doors to the personality.

Socrates said that the first law was "Know thyself!" Graphology uniquely answers the need to know oneself. From our own point of view we can recognize three different "selves": the self we show off; the self we think we know; and the total self that too often remains unknown. Not to know oneself is intolerable, foolish and unnecessary.

I analyze psychiatric patients' handwriting to help identify the basic problem traits and determine what possible changes can be made. This helps introduce basic questions for the psychoanalyst and it offers a departure point for therapy.

Some of the earliest graphological research was done on the handwriting of mental patients. It was clearly demonstrated that the handwriting of schizophrenic patients showed significant differences from the handwriting of others. It was also discovered that as these schizophrenic patients were treated, their progress was clearly revealed in their handwriting.

This connection with psychiatry should not be too surprising. The early French and German schools of graphology in the 19th Century were developed and supported by psychologists. Without medical training it is unwise for the analyst to actually diagnose cases, but the teaming of psychiatry and graphology is a natural and productive partnership.

QUESTIONED DOCUMENTS

More familiar to the public, perhaps, is the field of forensic graphology. Experts in this field are widely used to determine the validity of "questioned documents" (possible forgeries.) Techniques for identifying handwriting have developed over the centuries to such an extent that it is now safe to say that a person's written word is truly his bond. The widespread use of graphologists in business and law has brought even more certainty to the meaning of a signed document. Due to intensive scientific inquiry and research, the strokes in a person's handwriting have become as identifiable as his fingerprints.

I am a charter member of the World Questioned Document Association. In today's business environment, contracts are of supreme importance. Whether we realize it or not, we daily sign many contracts and pledge our word through our writing — in the form of personal checks, credit card receipts, correspondence, etc. The contract is the foundation of the free economy.

In my work with a leading Minneapolis department store I see many cases of charge account customers refusing to pay their bills because they claim someone stole their card or used it without permission. Often the circumstances lead to some suspicion. In such cases the store acquires for me a sample of the customer's own handwriting. My job then is to compare this sample with the signature on the sales slip. Either the store investigators are very thorough or people are less honest than I thought they were, but in most cases I find that the customer's handwriting matches the signature on the sales slip. (It's usually because the cardholder didn't want to pay the bill and thought that claiming forgery was a simple way out of it.)

There is a difference between a *forgery* and *disguised writing*. A forgery is an attempt to duplicate the exact handwriting style of another person. Disguised writing is an attempt by an individual to mask his own handwriting style, often for purposes of fraud. What do I look for in disguised writing and forgeries?

- Differences in the pressure or heaviness of writing
- Measurements
- Speed of writing
- Rhythm of writing
- Size of letters
- Slant
- Alterations or patches
- Control of the hand by the brain
- Repeated strokes

It is not usually difficult to discover a forgery or disguised writing. Forgers will always do some of the habitual things, no matter how hard they practice or try. Even tracing a signature will betray a slower execution of the writing. When people try to disguise their handwriting they usually try to change the slant of their writing, but this doesn't matter. Writing with the opposite hand doesn't work, either. No matter how hard you try, you cannot completely disguise your own handwriting. It is an integral part of your personality. It is a complex of behaviors that originate in the brain; we could accurately describe handwriting as **"brain-writing."**

Most often the questioned documents examiner is only dealing with petty crime, but once in a while much more than that is at stake. In 1985, just before an American-Soviet summit meeting in Geneva, an ordinary Soviet seaman jumped ship in New Orleans. Miroslav Medved apparently had decided to defect to the United States.

Early in the evening of October 24, 1985, Medved jumped overboard as his cargo ship was waiting to be loaded with American grain. He swam ashore and immediate asked, through a written message, to be taken to the police (Fig. 6 Exhibit 2.)

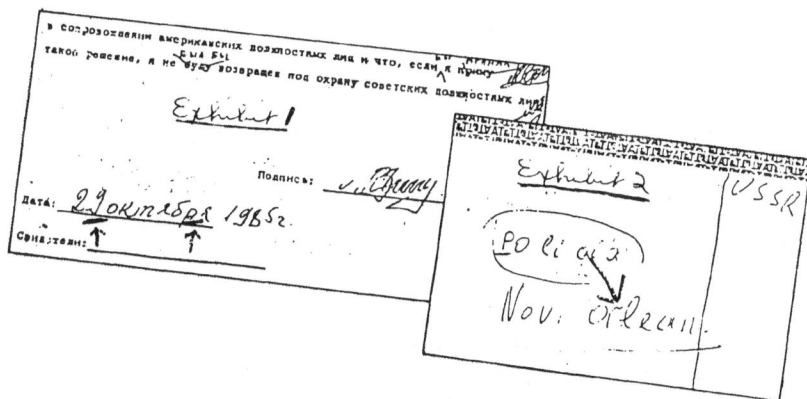

Fig. 6: *Two handwriting samples taken from the seaman identified as Miroslav Medved. (New York Times, March 2, 1986)*

In Exhibit 2, on the right, Medved wrote on the back of an envelope that he was from the Soviet Union (USSR), and that he wished to be taken to the police (policia) in New Orleans (Nov. Orlean) as soon as possible.

To communicate with Medved, the Border Patrol in New Orleans called a Ukranian interpreter (Medved spoke fluent Ukranian) who spoke by phone with the apparent defector for over 90 minutes. During this conversation, Medved told the interpreter, "I am very much afraid of what will happen to me."

For reasons that are not all clear, the Border Patrol decided to return Medved to his ship. As the harbor boat approached the Soviet vessel, Medved once again jumped into the Mississippi and tried to swim for shore. He was finally fished out of the water "wildly fighting — kicking and punching." When finally he was subdued, he was in despair and began banging his head against some rocks. In spite of this behavior, the authorities handcuffed him and returned him to the Soviet ship.

When the State Department later learned of the incident, high officials were understandably angry. This was not how the United States traditionally handled requests for asylum. The authorities finally insisted that Medved should be turned over to Immigration and Border Patrol officials to be interviewed again. President Reagan even suggested that the United States would use force to free the sailor if he was not allowed to speak openly on neutral ground.

A sailor was finally released by the Soviet ship for questioning, but something was clearly wrong. This sailor was cocky and belligerent. He spoke Ukranian badly and made disparaging comments about the United States. What was going on?

The answer may have been provided by two independent handwriting analysts. When Medved jumped ship the first time, he wrote his message in Russian on the back of an envelope **(Fig. 6, Exhibit 2.)** After his release for questioning, the sailor signed a statement taken by the State Department **(Fig. 6, Exhibit 1)** in which he insisted he was returning to the Soviet Union of his own free will. Both handwriting analysts concluded that the samples were written by different people. The Soviets, it seems, had pawned off a "counterfeit Medved" on the American authorities.

Compare the two exhibits yourself. The writing in **Exhibit 1** is more *slanted* than the other sample and by comparison the letter spacing is *cramped*. The speed of writing is also different between these samples. Under magnification, the strokes in **Exhibit 1** are shaky and hesitant. **Exhibit 2** strokes are brisk and smooth.

The "n" in **Exhibit 1** (fifth letter from the left) is quite different from the small "n" in "Nov. Orleans" as written in Exhibit 2. The writing in Exhibit 1 also has considerably more ornamentation, appearing more "European" than the plain strokes of **Exhibit 2**. (The "European" tradition in handwriting is distinctive to the graphoanalyst.)

These are a few of the obvious differences between the two "seaman" samples.

Serving as an expert witness in questioned documents cases is a large part of my job as a handwriting analyst. I am often called upon to compare handwriting samples with signatures on a will. When wills go to probate, someone often will contest the legitimacy of the signature. In some cases, millions of dollars are at stake.

I particularly enjoy jury trials, which give me the opportunity to use large photostatic copies and projected transparencies to demonstrate the sometimes subtle differences in handwriting strokes. In one case, the compelling evidence was a small quirk: the way the forger dotted his "i's".

Relatively few handwriting analysts are allowed to testify in court regarding questioned documents cases. Special training and certification is required before "expert witness" status is bestowed. When teased out into high relief by an expert witness, the evidence provided by handwriting analysis frequently is the basis for the jury's final evidence.

GRAPHOTHERAPEUTICS

For me, **graphotherapy** is the most exciting use of handwriting analysis. **It is a system by which each of us can change personality traits that have been discovered in our handwriting. By modifying an individual stroke, we can modify the trait that is connected to it.** For example, if you discover procrastination in your handwriting (revealed by the failure to finish the crossing of your "t's"), don't give up hope. You can learn how to change that stroke, and by changing your handwriting you will change the way you think and live.

In this book we will be using actual handwriting samples to learn the basics of this fascinating technique. You will learn to look at your own handwriting (and the handwriting of those near and dear to you) for clues about what makes you special. But there is a lot of work ahead before you can take advantage of this wonderful tool. Fortunately, this work is great fun and full of personal revelations.

WHAT YOU WILL FIND IN THIS BOOK

Part II

This is a condensed reference manual that catalogs in an easy to use form the important strokes you will be looking for in your writing. It explains also how to use this information in a meaningful way. *This book cannot be a complete, comprehensive in-depth study of graphoanalysis. Such a study would take you years to complete. This book is aimed at providing you with the most important and useful tools so you can get on quickly with the business of self-improvement.*

This section will give you a basic inventory of handwriting strokes categorized by the Three Zones of writing (more about this later.) The inventory also provides a good tutorial on the methods used by professional graphoanalysts.

Part III

This part begins your journey into graphotherapy. Here you will find the Insight Personality Profile and complete instructions on how to map your personality and determine how to develop your strengths and diminish your weaknesses. In many ways it is the most important part of the book, because it will teach you how to take your life and your personality into your own hands—literally!

This section also provides an alternate method for pursuing your graphotherapy and answers many of your remaining questions about this exciting personal development tool.

PART II

INTRODUCTION TO PART II

Part II is a reference section containing invaluable information concerning "*primary*" handwriting strokes. It is not, of course, an exhaustive study, but rather an introduction to the key strokes you will want to search for when analyzing your own handwriting.

Even though you will use this section primarily for reference in the future, it is wise to read through it at this time. You will find yourself acquiring a basic understanding of graphoanalysis as you work through this material. It is not important to memorize it, but *please*, concentrate on grasping the underlying principles.

The first basic principle is this: even though you will find personality traits listed alongside letters of the alphabet, the letters themselves are not important. These character traits are really attached to the STROKES that make up each letter, and several different strokes may be contained in the letter itself.

To help eliminate confusion, I have chosen to avoid listing the letters in alphabetical order. Instead, you will find the letters assembled into three distinct groups: the *Upper Zone* letters; the *Middle Zone* letters; and the *Lower Zone* letters. The letter "b" for example, is an upper zone letter because the stem of the letter protrudes upward into the "upper zone." The letter "o", on the other hand, is a middle zone letter because no part of it extends into the upper or lower zone. This organizational strategy stresses the importance of *strokes* within each letter and places less emphasis on the alphabet.

Any catalogue of strokes and related personality traits inevitably produces some duplication when displayed according to letters of the alphabet, and yet this organization is the most useful to you in making future analyses. I apologize for the occasional repitition, but it does serve a worthwhile purpose: it helps to reinforce the basic concepts and strokes that are the foundation of graphoanalysis.

To properly analyze a handwriting sample you must have at least one page of writing. A small sample may produce only a single occurrence of an important stroke and this is not adequate for a thorough analysis. If a particular stroke turns up only once or twice it indicates the *potential* for that given personality trait; to be considered definite, it must show up at least eight to ten times in the sample. If the trait involved is a *Red Flag* (more on this later), you will be on the alert to see if something serious is developing. The intricacy of handwriting analysis will become more evident when we tackle actual samples later on.

Right now, before you read the information in Part II, it is important for you to create your own handwriting sample. Please do this now by following the instructions below.

CREATE YOUR OWN HANDWRITING SAMPLE

You are ready to embark on one of the most exciting journeys of your life — discovering who your inner self is through handwriting analysis. As in all journeys, there must be a beginning. For this one, the beginning is your handwriting.

Sit down at a table. Do **not sit in an easy chair and write on your lap. Use the kind of pen you are familiar with and write at least one-half page on** unlined paper and another one-half page on lined paper.

There is a sample on page 86 of what you should write. Write this down word for word. It includes all the letters needed for the graph. Do not print. (Printing is much more difficult to analyze. You will use this handwriting sample as the basis for discovering the "inner you." Later in this book you will be shown how to find and interpret each of the *Power Strokes* and *Red Flags* that appear in your writing.

When you've finished writing this sample, you'll probably look at it and wonder where in the world to begin your analysis. Don't worry. This book is your personal guided tour into your personality. At the appropriate time you will be guided through the process of graphing your own character traits. This process will help you visualize the "inner you" just as a mirror helps you visualize your external appearance. You may be surprised to learn that you have literary ability... a keen, perceptive mind... a wild imagination.

This mirror to your inner self is called **"The Insight Personality Profile."** Once completed, it will reflect the "you" that no one else can see... and that you sometimes even hide from yourself! You may discover hidden talents or forgotten strengths. Through special writing exercises you can work to develop these positive traits and minimize any negatives that turn up. You can change your life!

As you read this, you may be saying to yourself, "This will never work. It seems impossible." That kind of attitude reminds me of the man who walked into a dark room and said to himself, "I'll never be able to see in here. It's too dark." Interestingly, next to the man was a light switch. And in your hands right now is a tool for illuminating your inner self. All you have to do is flick the light switch. Take the pen in your hand. Write a sample of your own handwriting. And then... proceed!

THINKING PROCESS

If you have not completed the handwriting sample as explained above, please do so before reading on.

In the pages to follow, many different personality traits will be identified and discussed. Perhaps none of them is so important as the traits that define one's "thinking processes." Each of us tends to think in a particular way: intuitively, logically, analytically, etc. Identifying the kind of thought process that best characterizes a handwriting subject is at the core of graphoanalysis. The way we think has a great bearing on many of our other characteristics.

You will find the following types of thinking processes mentioned many times throughout this book. In short, this is what the labels mean.

INTUITIVE

A person who thinks intuitively has a sense of "knowing" without explanation of where the information came from. The intuitive thinker is able to interpret things with no apparent effort. Intuition is the "sixth sense" that guides its possessor; it is a gift that should be developed.

ANALYTICAL

If you think analytically, you think more or less like a computer. You have the ability to analyze problems, sort out facts, break apart information and arrive at the best solution based on the accumulated data. You put problems in their proper perspective after evaluating systems and procedures.

LOGICAL

The logical thinker is a strategist, carefully planning ahead before making any move. If you think this way, you study each phase of a problem and the alternative steps to solutions in order to weigh the consequences of each. Only when you are satisfied with the plan will you act.

EXPLORATORY

A person who possesses exploratory thinking loves to delve into the unknown in search of discoveries. This breeds skepticism about others' conclusions until the facts have been gathered first-hand, usually with gusto. New horizons stimulate the mind of such a thinker.

KEEN COMPREHENSION

A person with keen comprehension can quickly grasp ideas and concepts. Often this provokes an impatience with people who give long explanations because a quick mental grasp of the idea already exists without such detail. This person has a penetrating mind that can easily order facts into conclusions.

MULTIPLE CHOICE

This is not a thought process, but an important point I want to make. It is possible to have a blend of several of these thought processes in one person — perhaps yourself — so don't be surprised if you find strokes suggesting this. Usually, however, one kind of process will dominate. Sherlock Holmes, for example, may have possessed all five of these thinking processes. Which one do you think would have been dominant? (If he had actually lived, we could tell from his handwriting!)

SLANT

Studying the "slant" of a handwriting sample can give the graphoanalyst an angle on the basic personality of the writer. Slant provides the first impression, and what a useful impression it is. Look at your own handwriting sample. It offers many clues about how you **emotionally** respond to life — not evidenced through physical acts, but in your mind. Many people are surprised and enlightened about their own emotional response pattern when they discover it through measuring the slant of their handwriting.

Yes, I said surprised and enlightened. Many of us don't know ourselves as well as we think. We are guilty of self-deception and judging our own personalities by our outward actions. When we unmask the way we *truly* respond to life through our emotions, the revelation can be quite startling.

Yes, I also said *measuring the slant*. General impressions are fine, but sometimes deceiving as well. I have seen writing that looks like it leans to the left (backhand) but actually slants right when measured! There is so much valuable information to be gleaned from the slant of our handwriting that we cannot simple "eyeball" it and call it good. Measuring the slant fortunately is not difficult. It is, however a process that demands precision. And patience... which will be amply rewarded by personality insights. Here's how you measure slant:

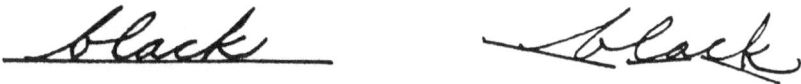

Fig. 7: Left, a single baseline drawn beneath a word. Right, three baselines drawn beneath an uneven word.

First, draw the **baseline** of each word with a ruler. This is the line (or lines) on which the middle zone strokes rest. It is a line from which a letter first rises and to which it then returns.

Don't be deceived by lined paper. Most handwriting does not actually use these printed lines as a baseline. Each word must still have its own baseline drawn. Some words, as in the example above, are written so unevenly that more than one baseline must be ruled. Remember that the accuracy of the subsequent measurement depends on these ruled baselines, so take your time and be precise.

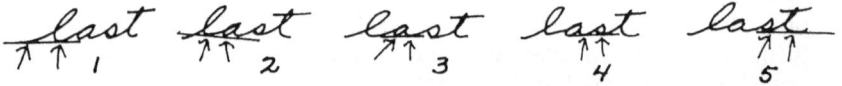

Fig. 8: Five baseline examples.

Study the baseline examples above. There are five baselines drawn for the word "last". Baseline #1 deals with the letter "1". Note where the baseline is drawn — where the "1" stroke first *leaves* the baseline and then comes down to touch it again (see arrows.)

Baseline #2 concerns the first part of the letter "a". See how the beginning stroke leaves the baseline and comes back to it (see arrows.)

Baseline #3 is drawn for the *completed* "a". The baseline touches the bottom of the loop and then the lowest part of the "a's" final stroke (see arrows.)

Baseline #4 begins by touching the lowest part of the final "a" stroke (which may also be considered the initial stroke of the "s".) The lowest point of the downstroke is the baseline's second touch point (see arrows.)

Baseline #5 is drawn from the second touch point of the "s" to the lowest point of the "t's" downstroke (see arrows.)

Fig. 9: A word after the upstrokes have been "lined" for measurement.

The second part of measuring slant concerns the upstroke. Draw a straight line over every upstroke as in the example above, but please pay strict attention to this instruction or your measurements will be wrong: every drawn line should start where each upstroke *begins to rise* from the baseline; the line should be drawn through the point at which the upstroke *has just begun to descend* toward the baseline.

It is critical to accurately identify the two points through which this line is drawn for each upstroke. I make a practice of making two visible dots for each upstroke, one marking the low point and the second marking the high point. With a ruler, I then carefully draw a straight line between these two dots.

Continue to "line" the sample until you have enough slants for an adequate analysis. A dozen is too few; a hundred or more is better. For a quick perspective, prepare to measure thirty upstrokes.

PRESSURE GUIDE

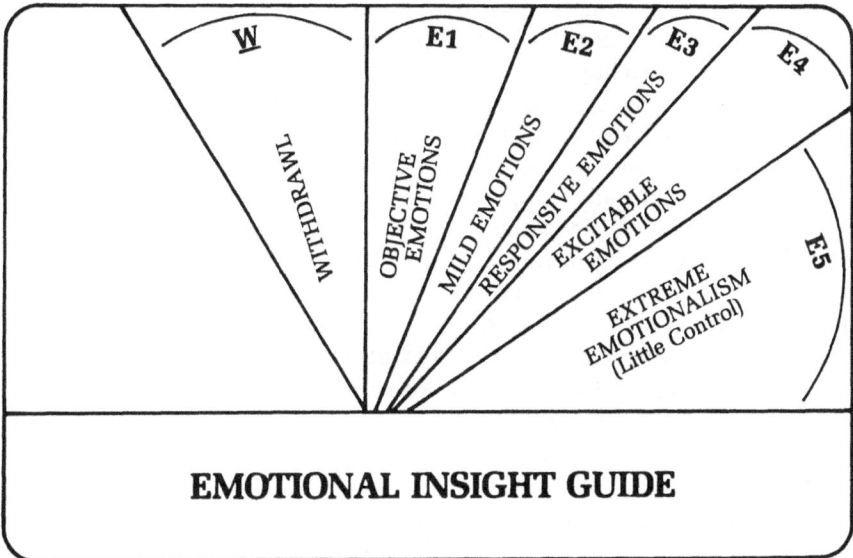

Fig. 10: The slant gauge aids in the measurement of emotional response.

Last, measure the slant of each upstroke against the slant gauge above. The *Apex* for each diagonal line on the gauge is the point at which that line touches the baseline. Likewise, the *Apex* of each upstroke is where the drawn measurement line meets the baseline.

Make sure the baseline of each stroke is critically aligned with the baseline on the gauge. Line up the *Apex* and baseline of the gauge with the *Apex* and the baseline of the stroke.

Fig. 11: *Measuring the "t" upstroke.*

As you measure the slant of the "t" above, notice that the dotted line falls within the space marked "E4" on the gauge. Write "E4" above the "t". Measure all of your lined strokes in this same manner, then determine the *average* slant of the sample.

That's it! I know it's a bit tedious — I have spent hundreds of hours measuring slants — but when you are done with a sample you have identified one of the cornerstones of personality analysis: emotional response.

As a rule of thumb, if your writing slants far to the right you are impulsive and quick to act on emotion. If, however, judgment generally rules your actions rather than emotion, you probably write more vertically.

No one, of course, exhibits the same emotional response all the time. That's why we look for the **majority** of **category** measurements in slant measures; it reveals a subject's basic emotional response pattern. Don't worry if your writing occasionally slants in different directions. It only proves you are human.

Slant analysis can be especially useful when applied to those who are close to us. It helps us understand them better and key into their emotional lives. But always remember, the measuring of slant must be done accurately or the analysis can be deceiving.

Here is a synopsis of the emotional response traits for people with the various slant averages:

E1

The "E1" personality writes vertically, or nearly so. For this person, judgment rules everything else. This is not to say the "E1" is unemotional. In an emergency, however, the "E1" stays calm and collected, expressing emotions later.

E2

This person has just a bit more right-hand slant than the "E1". Likewise, the "E2" is more easily aroused emotionally. Even though emotions are nearer the surface, the "E2" slant is almost never carried away by impulse. Emotions are under control.

E3

Here is a person who is quick to respond emotionally. Impulses are acted upon almost immediately. The "E3" is often the life of the party but still maintains a sense of objectivity, being careful not to be totally overcome by emotional feelings.

E4

This person is emotionally impulsive with just a residue of control. The "E4" has the ability to excite others with enthusiasm and makes a superb salesperson, actor, speaker. Such a person tires easily, however, like a hot flame that can burn only so long without refueling.

E5

A writer whose slant averages "E5" will have extreme emotional reactions to many things... and very little control. Perhaps you've heard the terms "hair-trigger" or "powder keg." Emotions here are almost always on the verge of breaking loose, both positively and negatively.

W

The true backslant writer is an introvert, a very private person who is Withdrawn ("W") in social situations. The "W" writer is seeking self-protection from hurts both real and imagined. A "backhand" writer often has been deeply hurt psychologically and now distrusts others, preferring to be alone.

VARIABLE

We all have some variation in slant, but a rare few have a truly "variable" slant; no detectable pattern and a meaningless "average" slant. Such a person, as you might expect, is hard to understand and unpredictable from day to day or even episode to episode.

Remember, the way a person responds emotionally may not always be acted out in behavior. Many of us have learned to hide our emotional reactions from others, and some of us are adept at masking them even from ourselves. That's why an accurate measurement of slant is so important. It reveals the true emotional response pattern of the writer. In some cases a mismatch of emotional response and behavior forecasts trouble. An "E5" who seldom *behaves* emotionally, for example, is damming up a swell of emotion that sooner or later may burst the dam in a torrential outbreak.

Here's a memorable way of characterizing the meaning of different slants. A forward slant indicates a reaching out to others and to the future. A vertical slant reveals a triumph of the conscious mind over present situations. A backslant shows a reaching back to the past, a retreat from others.

HEAVINESS

Once you've accurately measured slant, there is another determination that must be made: the *heaviness* of the writing. This is sometimes called "depth" or "pressure." It refers to the relative pressure with with the writing strokes are made. For simplicity, we'll divide heaviness into three categories: heavy, medium and light.

Fig. 12: An example of HEAVY handwriting.

Heavy

Heavy pressure writers are sensuous people. Their sense of sight is often heightened so that they enjoy color and composition. They greatly enjoy music (although musical taste remains highly personal.) Touch is important to "heavy writers", too; their personal surrounding are often filled with different textures to excite the tactile sense. They are extra-sensitive to fragrances and drawn to fine foods and interesting (sometimes exotic) tastes. The "heavy writer" loves good living and remembers experiences, integrating them deeply into his or her personality.

Fig. 13: An example of MEDIUM handwriting.

Medium

Sensual experience has less impact on the medium pressure

writer. When a sensual experience reaches them, they may soon forget it. **Emotional** experiences, however, are a different story, and each new one tends to crowd out what has gone before, even if the previous experience was negative. This means, of course, that emotional experiences leave little lasting impression on the "medium writer" even though, at the time they occur, they seem to be a dominant force upon the personality.

light

Fig 14: *An example of LIGHT handwriting.*

Light

The light pressure writer does not have highly developed senses or any profound depth of feeling. Unnecessary details are ignored by this person. Emotional experiences are more transitory and often not absorbed. The "light writers" have less force of personality, seldom harbor a grudge, and are rarely prejudiced because past experience holds so little sway over them. When a hurt or disappointment arrives, this person typically shrugs and says, "Tomorrow's another day."

HANDWRITING ZONES

If you've made it this far, you may be wondering just how "spooky or weird" this graphoanalysis stuff is going to get. Well... not very. You are not entering the Twilight Zone, but a section I call "Handwriting Zones." The bulk of this section contains invaluable information you'll want to read and look them up later. And the information is all filed under three main headings... the three "Handwriting Zones."

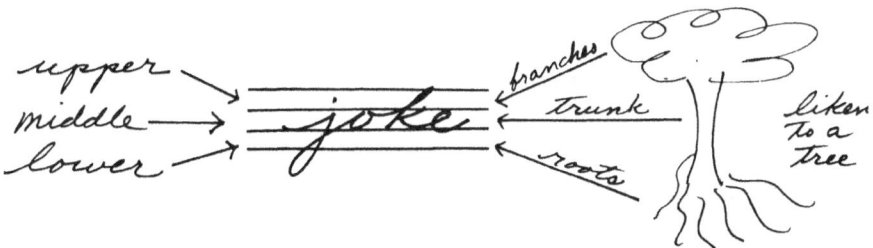

Fig. 15: *The Three Handwriting Zones*

The Middle Zone

Certain letters of the alphabet are called "middle zone" letters because they have no ascenders or descenders, no strokes that poke up into the "upper zone" or dangle into the "lower zone." When written, these letters are *a, c, e, i, m, n, o, r, s, u, v, w, and x.*

The vowels — except "sometimes y" — are found in this middle zone. If I were to caption this zone with a helpful generalization, it would be this: **"represents daily living and activities."** Not the letters themselves, of course; they only represent sounds. But generally, letters in this zone contain strokes that relate to personality traits having to do with daily living and activities. It is in many of these "middle zone" strokes that we express our day-to-day reactions and adaptations to living with each other.

The Upper Zone

This is the domain of the letters that majestically sail through our handwriting like the masts of tall ships. The "upper zone" letters are: *b, d, f, h, k, l, and t.* These strokes that reach toward heaven define the lofty world of religion and ethics in our personalities. If I were to generalize about this zone, it would be: **shows our spiritual, intellectual and imaginative side.**

The Lower Zone

This quintet of long-legged letters beats quite a different rhythm. The members are: *g, j, p, q, and z.* The small but lively group, in general: **reveals the earthly and material sides of our natures.** This is where we express — in code that graphoanalysis can decipher — the instinctual, physical, sexual part of our inner selves.

PRIMARY TRAITS

Each basic stroke in the following inventory is one which identifies, all by itself, a *primary* personality trait. A personality is made up of much more than these primary traits, however. Some traits (called **"evaluated traits"** by graphoanalysts) **cannot be identified by a single stroke.** These more complicated traits must be found by considering several primary traits together. Here are three simple examples:

DIGNITY + PRIDE = SELF ESTEEM

SECRETIVENESS + ANALYTICAL THINKING = CUNNING

SARCASM + PESSIMISM = CYNICAL

"Evaluated traits" become quite complicated; we will not deal with them directly. If you become interested in studying these traits, a thorough theoretical approach to them is available in the works of Milton N. Bunker and the publications of the International Graphoanalysis Society. A glance at the bibliography will give you some more avenues for exploration, but for now we will address the primary traits in a useful way.

The following inventory does not contain an exhaustive list of primary traits. Instead, I have culled through such a list and included here the most important and enlightening ones. These should answer most questions about yourself and guide you into galvanizing your strengths and excising your weaknesses.

MIDDLE ZONE LETTERS

SELF-RELIANCE. This stroke is unrelated to an individual letter so I'm listing it here. When you see a word or name underlined, it indicates self-reliance. Also, *any creative flourish* under a name or word indicates this trait. If a reversing stroke underlines the word, however, it must be made *in the manner illustrated* — that is first going to the left and then reversing directions ending up going to the right — to count as self-reliance.

SELF-CASTIGATION. *Every middle zone letter* can exhibit this stroke, so we're including it ahead of the letter-by-letter inventory. When a middle zone letter ends a word, look for a backlash stroke like this. The stroke must point back toward the beginning of the word. When you see this stroke, it reveals a writer who punishes himself or herself and does not appreciate his or her own worth.

DESIRE FOR ATTENTION. Watch the final stroke of a word for this trait. Look for a stroke that begins by pushing out to the right, then turns up **almost** as if it is going to become SELF-CASTIGATION (above) but stops short of curling back to the left.

TENACITY. A "hook" on the *end* of any stroke indicates tenacity. (Do not confuse this with the "acquisitive" hook that only occurs at the beginning of a stroke.)

CAUTION. Long, straight final strokes at the end of words, or straight dashes at the end of lines, indicate caution. If these strokes are found in majority, it reveals too much caution.

THE LETTER "a"

As a reminder, always measure the slant of a sample to determine the emotional responsiveness of the writer. And be sure to check for the relative heaviness of the pressure.

TALKATIVENESS. If there is an opening like this, it is an indication that the writer likes to talk. It's practically a build-in graphic reminder: a drawing of an open mouth.

RETICENCE. If there is no opening but the "a" is closed off instead, the writer probably is slow to speak. Outwardly, the writer is restrained and quiet.

BROADMINDED. A well-rounded letter reveals a person who is accepting of people and situations, and open to new ideas.

NARROW-MINDED. Narrow circles in the middle zone identify a writer who is limited in thinking and small in vision. This personality cannot easily accept the ideas of others.

SELF-DECEIT. A small loop on the left side of an "a" indicates self-deceit. This is a writer who is not fully facing reality. (When I see these strokes in a subject's writing I hesitate to use the emotionally charged term "self-deceit," instead relying on a more generous "not facing reality."

DELIBERATE SELF-DECEIT. An "a" with a small loop on both sides, like this, is evidence of a person who deliberately deceives. (Once again I prefer to use a more gentle assessment when identifying this trait.) This writer knows he or she is not facing reality. It is a conscious choice for which there may be many reasons. Facing reality, at some times, in our life — can be too painful so we choose to wait.

DIRECTNESS. When an "a" is missing an initial stroke, it indicates frankness or directness.

RESENTMENT. This all-too-common trait is revealed by a straight, inflexible initial stroke. This writer has the constant feeling of being taken advantage of.

SECRETIVE. If the downstroke of the "a" makes a little knot like this, the writer is not open to sharing secrets or personal matters.

ACQUISITIVE. Sometimes an "a" has this little hook at the beginning. This identifies a person who loves to "acquire" things, whether it's wealth, knowledge, collectibles, or something else.

Please note: an acquisitive hook (or any other stroke) that occurs only once or twice in a sample does not mean the writer definitely has the associated trait. Such an infrequent occurrence only means the writer has a tendency *toward that trait. To be a definite trait, the stroke must appear in the majority of writing you are looking at.*

THE LETTER "c"

DEPENDENT. An unnecessary initial stroke on the letter "c" (when it is the first letter of a word) is known as the "crutch" stroke. It indicates that the writer is dependent upon someone or something.

RESENTMENT. This trait is identified by a straight initial stroke as shown, as opposed to the bent initial stroke above.

THE LETTER "e"

BROADMINDED. When an "e" is fat and round like this, the writer is one who looks at life with a broader vision and listens to others.

NARROW-MINDED. An "e" that has a small and narrow loop indicates a writer who looks at life in a small and very limited way.

LITERARY INCLINATION and **PURSUE ARTISTIC AREAS.** This is one of the most positive indications in handwriting analysis. If a writer makes a "capital E" in the middle of a word where a lower case "e" should be found, that person is culturally minded. We call this letter shape a "Greek E." Such a writer loves literature and many of the finer things in life, and desires to improve in the loftier planes of thinking and living.

DEPENDENT. A capital "E" with a curved initial stroke, called a "crutch" stroke, indicates that the writer is leaning on someone or something for support.

RESENTMENT. When the initial stroke of a capital "E" is straight instead of curved, it suggests resentment.

THE LETTER "i"

IMPATIENCE. When the dot above the stem of an "i" looks more like a jagged line, the writer is easily annoyed or impatient.

IMPULSIVENESS. If the dot lands to the right of the "i", it is an indication that the writer is too quick to act without much thought.

PROCRASTINATION. If the dot lands to the left side of the "i", the writer is a procrastinator, putting off until tomorrow everything possible.

LOYALTY. A round, firm dot indicates loyalty. The writer believes what he says is true. Loyalty can be positive or negative, depending on who or what the loyalty is aimed at.

SELF-CENTERED. Dots that look like tiny circles are a sign of self-centeredness. This kind of dot can be found in the handwriting of people who consider themselves special and unique. Such people are often rugged individualists who often deviate from norms of dress and speech. (Jayne Mansfield, the actress, dotted her "i's" with tiny hearts.)

CONCENTRATION. In general, **small** writing is an indication of the ability to concentrate. Small "i" dots placed close to small "i" stems indicate an even higher concentration ability.

ATTENTION TO DETAILS. When an "i" is dotted directly over the stem, it means the writer pays close attention to details. Generally, this also means the writer will listen to people because close attention is paid to what they say. The closer the dot is to the stem, the more attention the writer gives to detail.

INATTENTION TO DETAILS. An "i" that is missing its dot altogether is evidence of a writer who is rushed or does not pay attention to details. It is possible the writer believes that some details do not merit attention.

THE LETTERS "m" AND "n"

The two letters, "m" and "n", reveal many of the same traits because of the similarity of the strokes.

LOGICAL THINKING, MANUAL DEXTERITY. If these letters are rounded on the tops, the writer has a logical mind, being able to gather facts and put them together in a rational, orderly way. This roundness also indicates that the writer can be skillful with his or her hands, often creatively so. Artists and musicians often exhibit this stroke.

KEEN COMPREHENSION;. "Needlepoint" tops show a mind capable of quick, keen comprehension. The longer and sharper these "needlepoints," the sharper the comprehension. Such a writer grasps ideas and understands concepts almost immediately.

ANALYTICAL THINKING;. Sometimes in the middle of an "m" you will find a shape that resembles "v". It occurs between the two humps. This "v" shape can also occur between the initial downstroke and the first hump in the "m" or "n". It indicates analytical thinking and reveals a writer who continually analyzes information to arrive at daily decisions. *Analytical thinking also strengthens all other mental processes that are present.*

EXPLORATORY THINKING;. A tent-like "m" or "n" reveals an exploratory mind at work. Such a mind moves out into the unknown with few preconceptions, eager for discovery. Think of these strokes as tiny mountain tops the explorer sets out to conquer.

DELIBERATE;. When the humps are spaced out like this, you are analyzing the handwriting of a deliberate mind. The writer is slow to come to decisions and slow to action. It does not imply less intelligence or laziness than others; this writer simply takes longer to get to his goals.

DIPLOMACY;. When the "m" or "n" slants *down to the right*, the writer is tactful or diplomatic. This is also a person who takes care in how he or she projects a personal image.

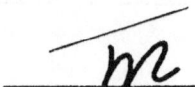

SELF-CONSCIOUSNESS; When the "m" or "n" slants *down to the left*, the writer is self-conscious, unduly aware of himself or herself, and uneasy in the presence of others.

REPRESSION;. When the downstrokes are almost completely retraced by the following upstrokes, the writer is suffering from repression. This person has erased unpleasant past experiences from the conscious mind, even though the subconscious retains the hurts or unpleasantness.

The initial stroke on a lead-off "m" or "n" can show some new traits as well as some we've seen before.

SENSE OF HUMOR;. A small curve or flair at the beginning of a lead-off "m" or "n" is what I like to call the "good humor" stroke. This is always great fun to find. The writer has a good sense of humor and can look at life in a light-hearted way.

TEMPER;. We all have a temper, but when a writer adds this little "temper tick" to his writing, you can be sure the boiling point is lower and the temper hotter than average.

RESENTMENT;. The straight-edge initial stroke betrays resentment in the writer.

ACQUISITIVE;. The "acquisitive" hook can also be found on the "m" and the "n".

LOVE OF RESPONSIBILITY;. On a beginning stroke, a closed loop that looks like a circle — as in the example — indicates a writer who is willing to do extra chores and accept more responsibility. The larger the loop, the greater is the writer's love of responsibility.

JEALOUSY;. A *flat-bottomed* loop in an initial stroke reveals jealousy. Do not confuse this stroke with either the "acquisitive hook" or the "love of responsibility loop" as described above.

DIRECTNESS;. A missing initial stroke shows directness of speech and expression.

THE LETTER "o"

TALKATIVENESS;. As in the "a", an opening at the top reveals a talkative writer. Also look for this trait in other letters having circular strokes.

RETICENCE;. A writer who does not like to talk or share thoughts with others usually closes off the "o" as in this example.

SELF-DECEIT;. An "o" may contain a loop inside the circle stroke on the left side only. This is a sign of self-deceit. The writer is not facing up to some truth in his or her life. The "o" can be open or closed at the top, depending on whether the writer is talkative or not.

DELIBERATE SELF-DECEIT;. A loop on both sides of an "o" indicates deliberate self-deceit, which may be a clue to look for things in the writer's life that are not being faced directly. If this stroke consistently appears, the writer should search for answers to "what" and "why" things are not being confronted.

BROADMINDED;. Such a person makes fat, well-rounded "o's", betraying a willingness to hear and consider the opinions of others.

NARROW-MINDED;. Skinny, cramped "o's" tell us the writer is narrow-minded, suffering from small-time thinking.

RESENTMENT;. An inflexible initial stroke on a lead-off "o" shows a resentful writer.

DIRECTNESS;. The absence of an initial stroke when the "o" is the first letter of a word indicates a writer who is frank, direct, saying things the way they are.

THE LETTER "r"

LOGICAL THINKING, MANUAL DEX-TERITY;. A flat-top "r", like the round-top "m" or "n", is indication of a logical thinking writer who is skillful and perhaps creative with his or her hands.

LITERARY INCLINATION, and **PURSUE ARTISTIC AREAS;.** An "r" that looks almost like a capital "E" (rocked slightly to the left) indicates a writer who finds the arts important. Refined living is important to this person.

ANALYTICAL THINKING;. Sometimes the upstroke forms a "v" shape that indicates a writer with an analytical mind.

KEEN COMPREHENSION;. If there is a point on the initial upstroke of an "r", you've found a good indication that the writer has keen comprehension.

THE LETTER "s"

IMPRESSIONABLE;. Sometimes an "s" is rounded on the top like this. A stroke like this indicates a writer who can be swayed easily.

KEEN COMPREHENSION;. The "needle-point" stroke at the top of an "s" shows keen comprehension. This writer is able to see the heart of an issue more quickly than others.

DECISIVENESS;. A firm final stroke on the last letter of word indicates decisiveness.

GENEROSITY;. Watch for a last stroke of a letter that is drawn out — at minimum, the width of the letter itself — before it curves upward. This stroke shows a writer who is generous.

THE LETTERS "u" AND "v"

ANALYTICAL THINKING;. Sometimes a "u" is written to look more like a "v". If the letter really is a "u", then the "v" shape indicates an analytical mind. (This is one of the few cases in which it pays to be able to read the language in which the handwriting is written, so the analyst knows whether the letter is a "u" or a "v".)

KEEN COMPREHENSION;. If the combination of the first upstroke and downstroke of a "u" comes out looking like the stem of an "i", it is an indication of a writer with keen comprehension.

RESENTMENT;. Watch for the straight resentment stroke preceding a lead-off letter.

THE LETTERS "w" and "x"

TEMPER;. The "w" leading off a word commonly shows the "temper tick" when this trait is present in the writer.

ANALYTICAL THINKING;. The "v" shapes that reveal an analytical mind often show up at the bottom of the letter.

EXPLORATORY THINKING;. The "w" is a good place to look for evidence of an exploratory mind, which shows up as an upside-down "v" shape in the center of the letter.

The "x" has little to offer the graphoanalyst who is looking for meaningful personality traits.

UPPER ZONE LETTERS

THE LETTER "b"

Remember, the "b" can indicate, by its slant and by the heaviness with which it is written, clues to the emotional life of the writer: how deep and long lasting his feelings are. Try measuring the slant of this stroke.

BASE LINE

PHILOSOPHICAL IMAGINATION;. The upper loop of the "b" is a clue to the philosophical imagination of the writer. The bigger the loop, the greater is the writer's concern about the deeper, philosophical questions of life. Always compare the size of the loop with the size of other writing.

DIRECTNESS;. As with many other letters, the absence of an initial stroke indicates directness and forthrightness in speech and expression.

TEMPER;. The "temper tick", a short straight initial stroke, is often found on the "b" when the writer possesses a tendency to become angry easily.

ACQUISITIVE;. When the "b" is the lead-off letter in a word, look for the acquisitive hook indicating that the writer has a tendency to acquire things: wealth, collectibles, knowledge, etc.

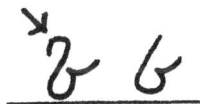

THE LETTER "d"

DIGNITY;. A "d" stem that is retraced — that is, contains no loop at all — reveals a writer with a sense of dignity. Stem must be **two** times higher than closest Middle Zone letters.

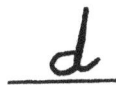

OVERLY SENSITIVE;. A fat, wide "d" loop shows a person who is sensitive about himself or herself. If this "d" stem loop is 1½ times or more the width of the closest middle zone letter, the writer is *overly* sensitive about his or her *appearance*. The fatter the loop, the more sensitive the writer.

LITERARY INCLINATION;. When a "delta d" like this shows up in handwriting, it reveals a person who is a writer or, at least, appreciates literature. This letter shape is called a "literary d."

STUBBORNNESS;. This tent-like "d" stem indicates stubbornness. The writer has difficulty yielding or obeying. Sometimes fear is the cause.

VANITY;. When the total "d" stem rises 2½ to 3 times the height of companion middle zone letters, you have a case of vanity on your hands.

INDEPENDENT THINKING;. If the upper portion of the stem is shorter than companion middle zone letters, it indicates a writer who thinks independently, free from influence.

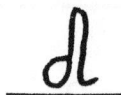

DELIBERATENESS;. When the upstroke and downstroke of the stem are separated, as in this example, it shows a writer who is careful and deliberate. This person is unhurried, methodical, and premeditated in his or her actions.

TALKATIVENESS;. Sometimes in the "d" you will find the unclosed circle shape that reveals a person who likes to talk.

THE LETTER "h"

PHILOSOPHICAL IMAGINATION;. Watch for the upper loop. The wider this loop, the bigger the imagination in the areas of philosophy, religion and abstract thought. A large loop like the example shows a search for wisdom, knowledge and ethical understanding. The loop must be 1 to 1½ times the width of companion middle zone letters.

INITIATIVE;. This "breakaway" stroke after an "h" reveals a writer with initiative. This person is always ready to take the first step.

KEEN COMPREHENSION;. These sharp "needlepoint" strokes indicate a mind capable of keen comprehension.

REPRESSION;. A *frequent* retracing of the downstroke shows "repression." This writer is holding in or repressing past experiences. Repression is an unconscious act that prevents the natural development of expression. It is a pushing away of thoughts instead of facing facts.

SUPPRESSION;. An *infrequent* retracing of the downstroke may indicate "suppression," the conscious, deliberate holding back of thoughts for definite reasons.

RESENTMENT;. A straight, inflexible initial stroke when an "h" leads off a word indicates resentment.

TEMPER;. Here is another example of the "temper tick" this time on a lead-off "h".

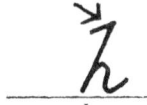

ACQUISITIVE;. The "acquisitive" personality may add this little hook to a lead-off "h".

DIRECTNESS;. As in so many letters, the absence of any initial stroke indicates directness.

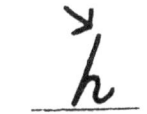

THE LETTER "k"

DEFIANCE;. If the "buckle" of the letter "k" is larger than companion middle zone letters, the writer is revealing defiance or a resistance to authority.

PHILOSOPHICAL IMAGINATION;. An exaggerated "k" loop reveals this trait. The wider the loop, the more philosophical imagination the writer possesses. (To qualify, the loop must be 1 to 1½ times wider than companion middle zone letters.)

THE LETTER "l"

The letter "l" is excellent for measuring slant. As you will recall, slant can give you an idea of how emotional the writer is. The

more the handwriting slants to the right, the more emotional and impulsive the writer is.

PHILOSOPHICAL IMAGINATION;. As in most upper zone letters, the loop indicates the degree of philosophical or abstract imagination. The wider the loop, the more imagination is possessed. (To qualify, the loop must be either 1 to 1½ times wider than companion middle zone letters.)

OVERBLOWN IMAGINATION;. An extremely fat "l" loop, like this one, shows an excessively broad concern with philosophical and abstract thought. This writer is apt to go overboard.

LIMITED IMAGINATION;. Narrow loops, on the other hand, show limited philosophical imagination.

LIMITED IMAGINATION;. Here is another way a writer betrays a limited philosophical imagination: tiny "l" loops barely taller than companion middle zone letters. This writer tends to think only of daily mundane matters.

EXPLORATORY THINKING;. Sometimes the "l" loop contains the "exploratory" stroke. In the "l" it appears as a pointed tip or upside-down "v" at the tope of the loop. In an "l", this stroke shows a writer who is eager to explore philosophical or abstract ideas.

DIPLOMACY;. Watch for "ll's" and "lt's" in words. When the tops slant *down to the right* — that is, when the top of the right-hand letter of the pair is shorter than the left-hand letter — diplomacy is indicated.

SELF-CONSCIOUSNESS;. This trait is revealed when the tops of "ll's" and "lt's" slant *down to the left*. This means that the left-hand letter is shorter than the right-hand letter.

THE LETTER "t"

How high are a writer's GOALS? This revealing bit of information is determined by where the "t" crossing is made. The higher up the stem, the higher the goals. The following illustration identifies five kinds of **GOALS**: low, limited, practical, high, and visionary.

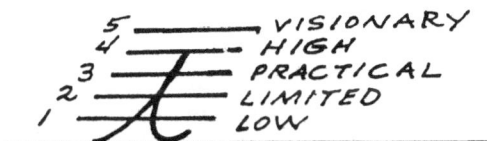

The "t" crossing also is directly tied into the trait of **SELF-CONFIDENCE**. High goals accompany high self-confidence. The following illustration labels four levels of this important trait.

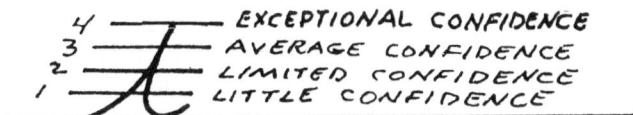

ENTHUSIASM;. The length of a "t" crossing is a relative measure of the writer's enthusiasm. A long, exuberant crossing shows great joy and enthusiasm in life. Some writer's even cross several "t's" with one stroke. These writers are exciting to be around!

OPTIMISM;. An upward slant to the crossing reveals an optimistic individual.

DOMINATING;. If the crossing slants downward and increases in heaviness to a blunt end, like this, the writer has a dominating personality. This is a person who rules and controls through his or her own ability.

DOMINEERING;. If the crossing starts out thick and slants downward tapering to a point like an arrow, the writer is domineering. This person is often arrogant and influences others easily with his will... even if there is no genuine ability to back it up.

SARCASTIC;. A *level* crossing that ends in a point on the right is evidence of sarcasm.

PROCRASTINATION;. When the crossing does not quite make it across the "t" stem, the writer is a procrastinator, putting off until tomorrow everything possible.

ANGER;. When the crossing is entirely to the right of the stem, not crossing it at all, you have found evidence of anger.

IRRITABILITY;. This trait is indicated by a "t" crossing that starts on the wrong side of the stem, and ends in a point.

SUPERFICIAL THINKING;. A bowl-shaped "t" crossing like this reveals superficial thinking. This is also a writer who is not putting forth a best effort, not living up to potential.

SELF-CONTROL;. A crossing that looks like an arch or umbrella indicates self-control.

STUBBORNNESS;. When the "t" stem forms a tent shape like this, the writer is revealing stubbornness.

WILL POWER;. A "t" crossing that is *thicker* then the stem indicates strong will power.

DELIBERATENESS;. A stem that shows an upstroke separated from the downstroke is evidence of a deliberate thinker, one who takes time to come to conclusions.

OVERLY SENSITIVE;. Sometimes a writer will make a loop out of the stem. A fat, wide "t" loop shows a person who is sensitive about his tasks and performance. If this "t" stem loop is wider than the closest "e" or "a", the writer is *overly* sensitive. The fatter the loop, the more sensitive the writer.

INDEPENDENT THINKING;. Stems that are only slightly higher than companion middle zone letters indicate independent thinking.

VANITY;. If the total "t" stem is more than 2½ times the height of companion middle zone letters, the writer shows vanity.

DIPLOMACY;. Watch for "tt's" and tl's" in words. When the tops slant *down to the right* — that is, when the top of the right-hand letter of the pair is shorter than the left-hand letter — diplomacy is indicated.

SELF-CONSCIOUSNESS;. This trait is revealed when the tops of "tt's" and "tl's" slant *down to the left*. This means that the left-hand letter is shorter than the right-hand letter.

INITIATIVE;. This kind of final "t", in which the last stroke pushes out, indicates initiative.

DECISIVENESS;. A final "t" that ends in a firm, blunt manner reveals decisiveness.

LOWER ZONE LETTERS

SELF-RELIANCE;. When you see a word or name underlined once, or underscored with flourish, or underlined with a reversing stroke going to the right, it indicates self-reliance.

TENACITY;. A "hook" on the *end* of any stroke indicates tenacity. (Do not confuse this with the "acquisitive" hook that only occurs at the beginning of a stroke.)

CAUTION;. Long, straight final strokes at the end of words, or straight dashes at the end of lines, indicate caution. If these strokes are found in majority, it reveals too much caution.

THE LETTER "f"

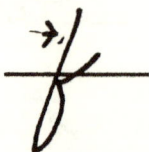

DIRECTNESS;. If the upper loop is missing on a lead-off "f" and there is no initial stroke, it shows that the writer is direct in speech. This writer also exhibits lack of philosophical imagination.

MENTAL BALANCE;. The letter "f" should be looked at closely for balance. If the upper and lower loops are the same size, it indicates mental stability and a balanced personality.

LITERARY INCLINATION;. Sometimes the **figure eight** can be found in the "f". This is called the "literary eight" and indicates ease of expression... a literary ability.

PERSISTENCE;. A little "tie" or "knot" that finishes up the stroke indicates persistence or enduring continuance. This stroke is a visual metaphor for its trait; it "ties up:" or finishes the writing of the letter. It shows a refusal to give up until completion.

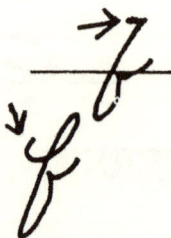

TEMPER;. The "temper tick" can be found also on lead-off "f's".

ACQUISITIVE;. On lead-off "f's", look for the acquisitive hook.

THE LETTER "g"

SECRETIVE;. If the circle stroke of a "g" is frequently closed, the writer is secretive and reserved in sharing thoughts with others.

FLUIDITY OF THOUGHT;. Figure eights in this letter show fluidity of thought or speech. "Fluidity" means that the thought processes are not rigid" all avenues are looked at easily. The figure eight is also called a "literary eight", indicating that the writer likes the refined life and probably has literary ability or great appreciation for literature.

MATERIAL IMAGINATION;. Large lower loops indicate material imagination. The material world is comprised of objects and sensual experiences. This includes our comforts and pleasures. The size of the lower loop tells us how much material imagination is present. The wider the loop, the greater the imagination. Compare the width to the closest Middle Zone letter.

RETICENCE;. When the circle shape above is closed, it reveals a person who is reserved or disciplined before speaking.

TALKATIVENESS;. An open circle shape indicates a person who likes to express himself or herself through speech.

BROADMINDED;. Fat, well-rounded circle shapes are evidence of a writer who is willing to listen to others' views without feeling threatened.

NARROW-MINDED;. Narrow, cramped-looking circle shapes indicate a narrow-minded person.

CLANNISH;. A tendency to be exclusive in relationships is shown by small lower loops, either round or squared off.

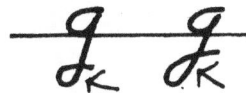

SELECTIVE;. A narrow lower loop reveals a person who is selective in choosing or keeping friends. The larger the loops, the wider the circle of friends.

DETERMINATION;. A heaviness or thickness of the downstroke shows good determination, a firm intention to do what needs to be done. The *length* of the stroke shows how long the writer will sustain that determination; the *heaviness* shows the strength of the determination. **Length and heaviness of this stroke must be judged in comparison to the other letters written.**

DETERMINED BUT UNIMAGINATIVE;. The "determination" downstroke (see above) without a lower loop reveals a writer who is determined but lacks imagination.

LACK OF DETERMINATION;. This trait is indicated by a lower loop that is barely begun before it is aborted.

UNDEVELOPED IMAGINATION;. Incomplete lower loops indicate an undeveloped imagination.

AGGRESSIVENESS;. A stroke that pushes out firmly from the downstroke indicates aggressiveness. This writer is full of enterprise, is bold and active, and is unafraid of acting.

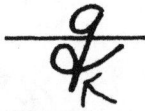

PERSISTENCE;. This written knot, called a "persistence tie," may be found on the"g". This writer shows an unwillingness to quit a job that is underway.

SELF-DECEIT;. An inside loop on the left side of the circle shape indicates self-deceit. This is a writer who is not fully facing reality but probably doesn't realize it.

DELIBERATE SELF-DECEIT;. A small loop on both sides of the circle is evidence of a person who deliberately deceives herself or himself. This writer knows about the deception. It is a conscious choice for which there may be some reason. Like painful past experiences.

THE LETTER "j"

NOTE: See the LETTER "i" for a discussion of the "i" dots and related traits. This information applies equally to "j" dots.

THE LETTER "p"

DESIRE PHYSICAL ACTIVITY;. This letter can give us a clue to the writer's desire for physical activity. The larger the lower loop, the greater that desire. This desire may only cause the writer to watch sporting events, but the tendency to be active still exists. The width of the lower loop must be wider than the closest "e" or "a".

DESIRE FOR CHANGE;. Unusually long downstrokes show a desire for change and variety. The further this stroke protrudes into the lower zone, the stronger this trait.

CONFUSION;. The downstroke can also be a sign of trouble if it begins to interfere with the writing on the line below. Any letter that does this indicates a person who is confused by too many interests.

TEMPER;. The "temper tick" may be attached to a lead-off "p".

RESENTMENT;. This letter can also contain the resentment stroke, a straight and inflexible initial stroke.

DIRECTNESS;. A lack of an initial stroke indicates frankness or directness.

EXPLORATORY THINKING;. This adventuresome thought process is revealed by the inverted "v" shape that sometimes occurs before the downstroke.

THE LETTER "q"

RETICENCE;. Closed circle shapes in this letter indicate a reticent, untalkative person.

TALKATIVENESS;. Open circle shapes show a gift of gab.

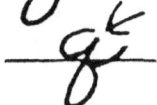

MATERIAL IMAGINATION;. As in other lower loop letters, the wider the loop, the larger the material imagination. The width of the loop must be wider than the closest "e" or "a" or "o".

BROADMINDED;. This admirable trait is evidenced by fat, well-rounded circles.

NARROW-MINDED;. Narrow, cramped circles indicate this less admirable trait.

PERSISTENCE;. The "persistence tie" may show up in the "q" if the writer has this trait.

SELF-DECEIT;. An unknowing failure to face reality is indicated by a loop on the left of the circle shape.

DELIBERATE SELF-DECEIT;. If a loop occurs on both sides of the circle, the writer is consciously deceiving himself or herself about something. Not completely facing reality about something in his or her life.

AGGRESSIVENESS;. A lower upstroke that breaks away sharply from the stem shows aggressiveness.

THE LETTER "y"

MATERIAL IMAGINATION;. The "y" is an indicator of material imagination. This has little to do with philosophical flights of fancy. This material imagination encompasses all of the practical, earthly activities we engage in every day. The wider the lower loop in the "y", the greater the writer's material imagination. The width of the loop must be wider than the closest "e" or "a" or "o".

LOVE OF VARIETY;. Besides revealing material imagination, a wide lower loop in a "y" shows the writer's love of variety and change.

LACK OF DETERMINATION;. This trait is indicated by a lower loop that is barely begun before it is aborted.

DETERMINATION;. The determined personality completes the lower loop begun by a strong, heavy downstroke. The length of the downstroke reveals how long the writer will maintain determination; the heaviness of the downstroke shows the strength of that determination. *This stroke must be judged in proportion to other written strokes.*

DETERMINED BUT UNIMAGINATIVE;. The determination downstroke without a loop suggests a writer who is determined but lacks imagination.

SELECTIVE;. A thin lower loop indicates the writer is very selective of his or her friends. The wider the loop, the wider the circle of friends.

CLANNISH;. A small lower loop, rounded or squared off, indicates a writer who is not convinced by words or deeds of the value of another person. The clannish person continually seeks out new evidence of the value of another person. It is difficult to get through to a truly clannish person.

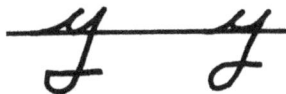

LITERARY INCLINATION;. The "literary eight" may occur in the lower zone of the "y" if the writer possesses either literary ability or an appreciation of literature.

AGGRESSIVENESS;. A stroke that pushes out firmly from the downstroke indicates aggressiveness. This writer is full of enterprise, is bold and active.

PERSISTENCE;. The persistence tie is often found in the "y", too. The writer shows an unwillingness to quit a job once begun.

THE LETTER "z"

MATERIAL IMAGINATION;. The "z" is also an indicator of material imagination. This has little to do with philosophical flights of fancy. This material imagination encompasses all of the practical, earthly activities we engage in every day. The wider the lower loop in the "z", the greater the writer's material imagination. The width of the loop must be wider than the closest "e" or "a" or "o".

DETERMINATION;. The determined personality completes the lower loop begun by a strong, heavy downstroke. The length of the downstroke reveals how long the writer will maintain determination; the heaviness of the downstroke shows the strength of that determination. *This stroke must be judged in proportion to heaviness in other written strokes.*

SELECTIVE;. A thin lower loop indicates the writer is very selective of his or her friends. The wider the loop, the wider the circle of friends.

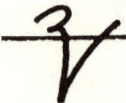

AGGRESSIVENESS;. A stroke that pushes out firmly from the downstroke indicates aggressiveness. This writer is full of enterprise, is bold and active.

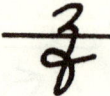

PERSISTENCE;. The persistence tie is often found in the "z", too. The writer shows an unwillingness to quit a job once begun.

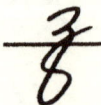

FLUIDITY OF THOUGHT;. Figure eights in this letter show fluidity of thought or speech. "Fluidity" means that the thought processes are not rigid; all avenues are looked at easily. The figure eight is also called a "literary eight", indicating that the writer likes the refined life and probably has literary ability or a great appreciation for literature.

HANDWRITING ANALYSIS

THE IN-DEPTH PERSONALITY PROFILE

There is much more to preparing an in-depth personality profile through handwriting analysis than skipping through the alphabet looking for certain strokes. It is more involved than blindly applying the meaning of a stroke to a given handwriting sample. Human beings are never so simple. Each of us is a complex combination of strengths and weaknesses, virtues and faults. Each individual personality trait is an adaptation made by the writer to the very personal experiences of living. Identifying a stroke in a handwriting sample is discovering a piece of evidence that must be analyzed in context with all the other evidence gathered. This is the kind of intensive evaluation that graphoanalysts and graphologists have been trained to provide.

THE INSIGHT PERSONALITY PROFILE

The **book** you are reading cannot hope to give you the information and training it takes to formulate an in-depth profile of yourself or someone else. It concentrates on **primary traits** revealed through single handwriting strokes. These traits, however, can give you a remarkable **insight** into a person you already know quite well: YOU! They can reveal characteristics you may be hiding from yourself. They can identify latent strengths and misunderstood virtues. They can also help you pinpoint specific weaknesses, faults and other potential targets for improvement.

In other words, this book **cannot** make you a professional graphoanalyst capable of scrutinizing the finer nuances of the human psyche. It can enable you, however, to overhaul your psychological engine and fine-tune your personality if you wish.

Before we move onto the exciting subject of graphotherapy, though, let's practice using some of the knowledge gained in this section. Following are a few handwriting samples of famous people. It's always fun to compare the strokes found in handwriting samples with the traits exhibited by the writers themselves... in this case, writers we all know something about.

FAMOUS PEOPLE

In this section you will get a feel for the practical side of handwriting analysis by checking out the writing samples of famous people. These people all have sharply defined public images, sometimes created by the media and sometimes by actual behavior. We will find, first of all, many contradictions between actual traits possessed and these public images. This is an intriguing aspect of graphoanalysis. We will also find that many of these successful people have the same POWER TRAITS.

In my career I have analyzed the handwriting of many public figures at their request. Often the response has been, "How could you have known that?" Public images today are so carefully built and protected that even painstaking research into the public record would not reveal what I have learned from handwriting samples.

For this section I have assembled a collection of handwriting from well-known people who have become controversial, beloved, even infamous. I've also included a few samples from people who are not famous but whose handwriting I came upon in a unique way. As you look at each of these samples, try to do some analysis on your own. It makes great practice. Then join me in a guided tour into some of the fascinating mysteries of the human personality.

SIRHAN AND THE KENNEDYS

Sirhan the Assassin

Robert F. Kennedy was born to a privileged life. His mother, Rose, the daughter of a famous Boston politician, was married to Joseph P. Kennedy, a very successful businessman in his own right. Robert soon found himself following in the footsteps of two rather extraordinary brothers. John Fitzgerald was to become President of the United States.

The years of the Kennedy administration were filled with style and grace. These were the "Camelot" years, too good to last. The end abruptly came when the charismatic President was cut down at the height of his powers by an assassin. Those closest to the younger Robert Kennedy during those years claim that the tragedy had a profound effect on his personality.

Then came 1968, a turbulent year in America's history. The Vietnam war already had split the nation's loyalties and a bitter presidential primary further divided an already fragmented Democratic party. Eugene McCarthy surprised everyone with a

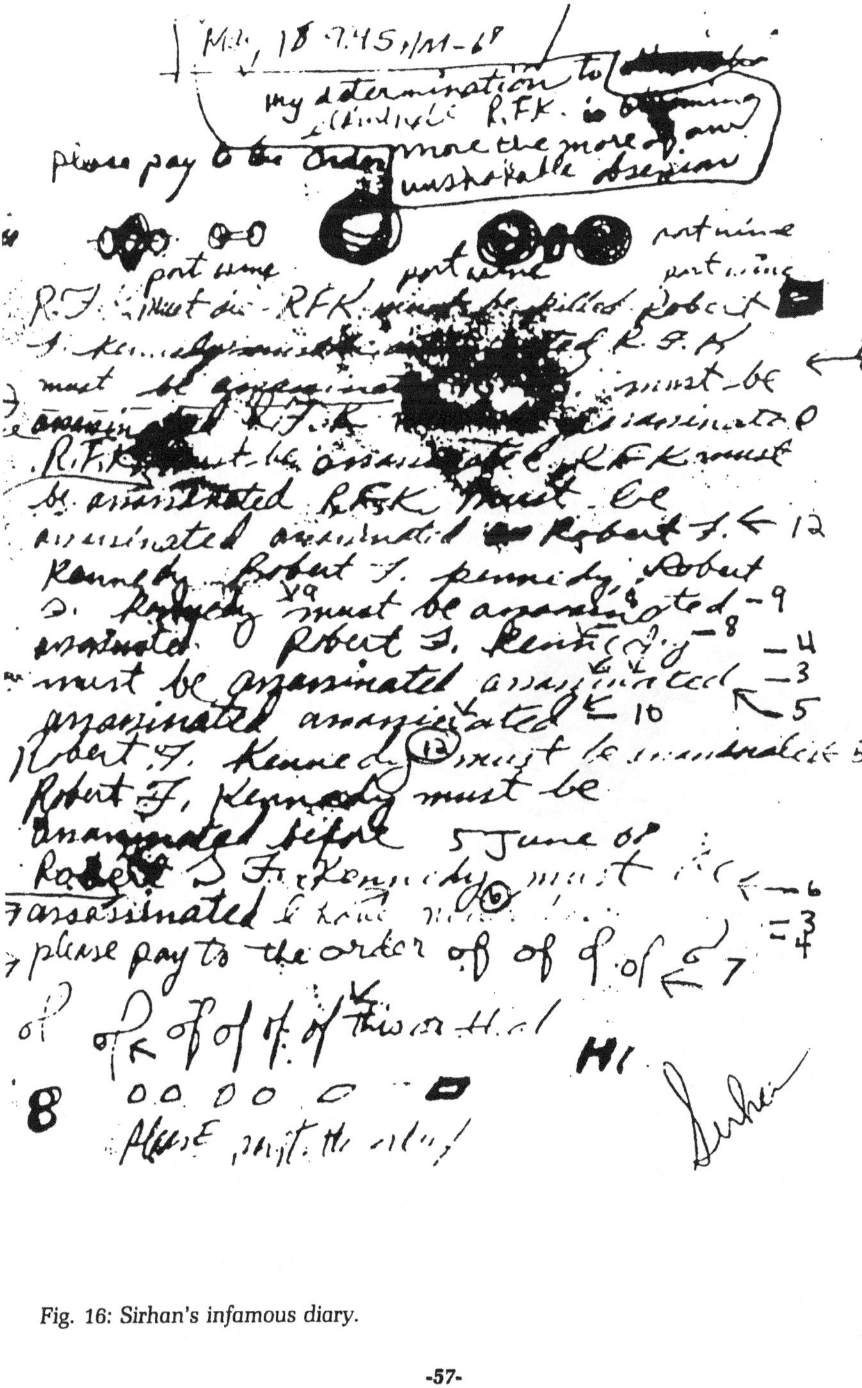
May 18 9.45 AM—68
my determination to [redacted]
eliminate R.F.K. is becoming
please pay to the order more the more of an
unshakable obsession
port wine
port wine port wine port wine
R.F. must die - RFK must be killed Robert
F. Kennedy must be assassinated R.F.K.
must be assassinated must be
assassinated R.F.K. must be assassinated
R.F.K. must be assassinated R.F.K. must
be assassinated RFK must be
assassinated assassinated Robert F. ← 12
Kennedy Robert F. Kennedy Robert
F. Kennedy must be assassinated —9
assassinated Robert F. Kennedy —8 —4
must be assassinated assassinated —3
assassinated assassinated ← 10 ↖5
Robert F. Kennedy (12) must be assassinated ← 5
Robert F. Kennedy must be
assassinated before 5 June 68
Robert F. Kennedy must be ←6
assassinated
please pay to the order of of of of ← 7
of of of of of of this or that
HI
8 0.0 0 0 0
Please pay to the order
Sirhan

Fig. 16: Sirhan's infamous diary.

strong showing in the New Hampshire primary. McCarthy's appeal to young voters and anti-war activists became a major theme of the Democratic campaign. Hubert Humphrey, considered a "hawk" and a surrogate of the President, was fighting an uphill battle to convince voters that he had a new vision for the country.

When Robert Kennedy entered the race, the Party outlook became stormier than ever. But on the evening of Robert's win in the California primary, June 5, 1968, history repeated itself. Another Kennedy was assassinated. This time the killer was a young Christian Arab who had grown up in Jordanian Jerusalem. The killer's name: Sirhan Bashara Sirhan.

At Sirhan's trial, the notebooks he had kept were introduced as evidence. In blotchy jottings, Sirhan had written over and over the words, "RFK must die, RFK must be killed."

This page from Sirhan's diary is a goldmine for the graphoanalyst. But before we look at some of strokes to be found here, look at the strange, messy blotches on this sample. If you stare at the four blotches in the vicinity of (1), something very eerie will occur. Together, these blotches form the picture of a hideous face. Some have called it the face of evil.

Fig. 17: A closer look at the "face of evil."

Well, this is no treatise on the occult. To the graphoanalyst, these messy blotches indicate extremely "muddy thinking." While the spots look almost like Rhorschach ink blots, they tell us the state of Sirhan's mind, not ours. At the time of the writing, Sirhan's thinking was **muddled!**

You have learned that a "t" crossed high on the stem indicates high goals; a crossing in the middle of the stem reveals **practical goals.** Look at Sirhan's "t's" (2): some are crossed at the middle and others at the top of the stem. Sirhan may have felt that his goal was high, but can murder truly be considered a high goal?

Sirhan had many of the necessary ingredients for an assassin. His handwriting shows that he was an excessive person with extreme **sensuality** in his thinking (slant, heaviness, large lower loops.) And the dot (3) of the "i" shows that this killer paid close **attention to details** (the closer the dot to the stem of writing, the greater attention to detail.)

Sirhan was loyal to his native country and quite intuitive. **Loyalty** is exhibited in the round way he dots his "i"(4), and we can see his **intuition** in the separation of so many letters (5). So even in his muddled mental state, Sirhan's intuition helped guide him into making his move at the right time.

Notice: the word "assassinate" almost jumps out at you from the page. The emphasis of this word, however, must be disregarded. In handwriting analysis the meaning of a word has no significance; only the strokes matter.

The length and width of Sirhan's lower "y" loops show that he had a good **material imagination** (6). He could easily imagine what he had to do, could pay attention to details and follow his intuition. This is a hard combination to stop.

Notice how Sirhan practices the phrase, "Pay to the order of... of... of..." (7). This is interesting: to forge a signature, the career criminal will often practice writing significant strokes or letters of the writing they wish to copy. The most difficult strokes to forge, however, are those which do not come naturally to the forger — the strokes which most contradict his or her own traits. The forger will have difficulty, for example, copying the handwriting of an honest person because the forger lacks that trait.

In this forgery practice routine, Sirhan's "f" strokes are particularly intriguing. You will recall that a balance between the upper loop and the lower loop indicates balanced thinking. As Sirhan began to practice, there was no balance between the "f" loops. His thinking was **unbalanced.** As the practice continued, though, he started writing more like the person he was copying; the "f" loops became more balanced, indicating a better balance in his own mind. This is a good example of a graphotherapy exercise. Unconsciously, Sirhan was affecting a small change in his mind by physically changing certain strokes in his writing.

Now look at Sirhan's "m's". The peaky humps indicate **exploratory thinking** (8). From the court record it can be learned that Sirhan explored all avenues, all possibilities for this assassination before acting. Also frightening is his excellent **manual dexterity** (9). This is revealed by the rounded "m's" and the "n's". Most likely he was not worried about handling the rifle.

What is so sad about Sirhan is that he had many talents. Used in another way, he could have been an asset to his country: a politician or writer. He even shows a degree of **sensitivity** (10) in some of his "d's".

Whenever an upper zone of t and d stroke is 2½ times higher than its companion middle zone letters, it indicates **vanity** (12). In this sample, Sirhan was revealing his belief that "I am the one to do this. I know I can do it!"

The way Sirhan makes round "i" dots shows **loyalty.** Unfortunately for all of us, Sirhan's muddled mind distorted this loyalty into something murderous and evil.

The Kennedy Plea for Mercy

Nine months after the death of Robert Kennedy, Sirhan Sirhan went to trial. He was convicted and sentenced to death in California. In imposing his sentence, the trial judge made note of a remarkable letter in which Edward Kennedy pled for mercy for the murderer of his brother. As you look at this letter you may be surprised to find some of the same handwriting strokes that are found in Sirhan Sirhan's notebook.

The handwriting samples of Edward Kennedy and Sirhan Sirhan are of two men whose lives were tremendously different, yet who possessed many of the same traits. We can see immediately that Edward Kennedy pays **attention to detail** (3). Notice the "i's" dotted directly above the stems; and notice also how round these "i" dots are, indicating **loyalty.** He is also **intuitive** (5): this is revealed by the spacing and separation of the letters.

Kennedy also has **practical goals,** and they remain practical all the way through his writing, as you can see by the "t" crossings in the middle of the stems. But pay attention to those crossings that begin to the right of the stem, missing it altogether. This is the **anger** stroke (14), betrayed in a plea for mercy. And there is also **resentment** here, indicated by the straight, inflexible initial stroke of the "m" (15).

The content of his letter shows that Edward Kennedy tried to set aside his emotions. Despite his understandable resentment and anger, Kennedy's **self-control** (16), revealed by the arch-shaped "t" crossings, helped him do what he thought was right.

Kennedy **writes heavily,** the strokes pressed down deeply into the paper. This shows a person who has deep feelings, who doesn't forget emotional experiences easily. While Edward Kennedy will never forget this part of his life, he is willing to forgive! This letter tells a great deal about Robert Kennedy's younger brother: his self-control, his loyalty, and his **persistence** (shown by the little "tie" of the "t" crossing.)

The "d's" also show he likes to talk, a necessary trait for a politician. A "d" open at the top of the circle stroke indicates **talkativeness.** This trait is more apparent in Kennedy's "d" than in his "a" or "o" where it might also appear.

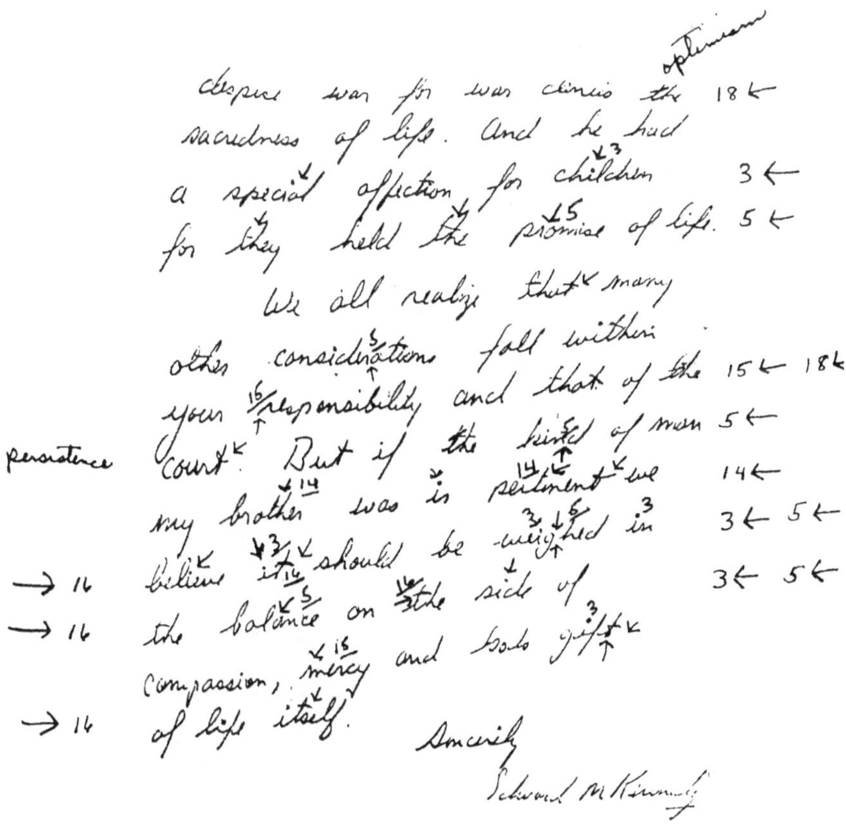

despise war for war denies the
sacredness of life. And he had
a special affection for children
for they held the promise of life.
We all realize that many
other considerations fall within
your responsibility and that of the
court. But if the kind of man
my brother was is pertinent we
believe it should be weighed in
the balance on the side of
compassion, mercy and God's gift
of life itself.
Sincerely
Edward M Kennedy

Fig. 18: Edward M. Kennedy's amazing letter to the sentencing judge at Sirhan's trial.

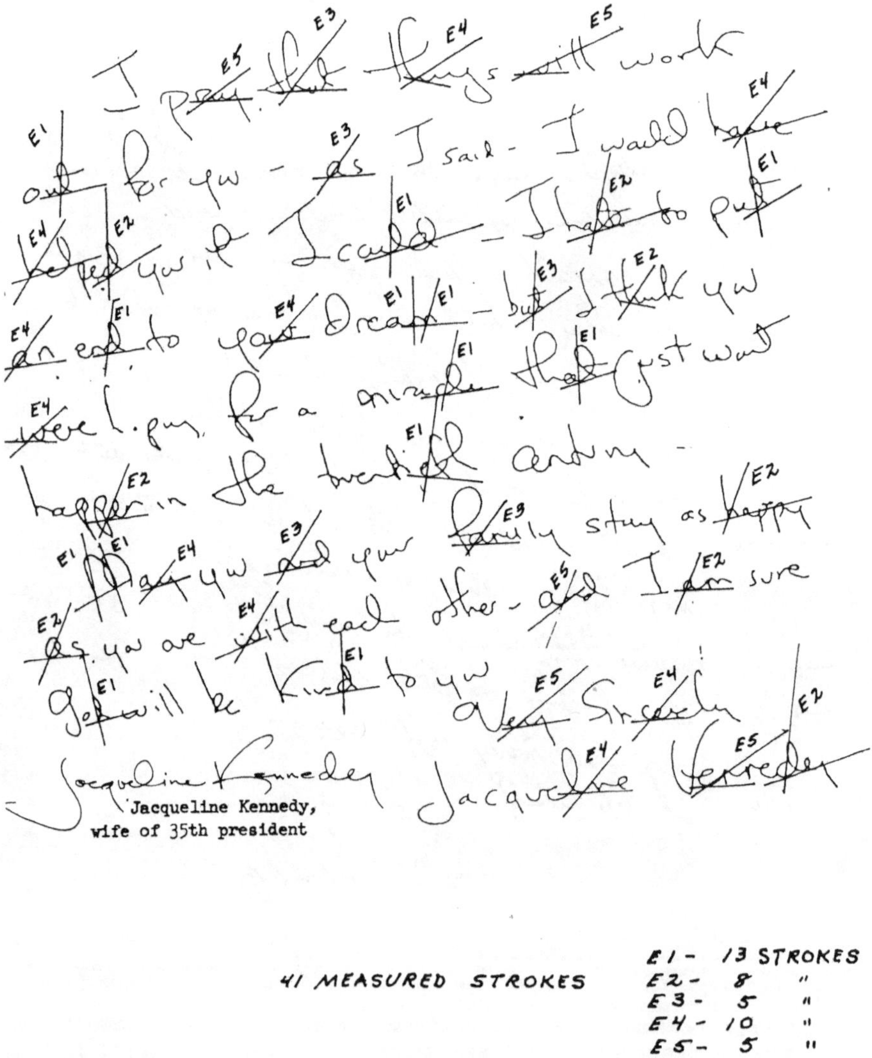

'Jacqueline Kennedy,
wife of 35th president

41 MEASURED STROKES

$E1$ — 13 STROKES
$E2$ — 8 "
$E3$ — 5 "
$E4$ — 10 "
$E5$ — 5 "

Last page of a handwritten letter signed by Jacqueline Kennedy to a begging stranger in England: "I pray that things will work out for you... I would have helped you if I could"

Fig 19: Jacqueline Kennedy Onassis' graceful, controlled handwriting.

Notice the "g" and "y". The unfinished lower loop with a strong downstroke indicates that he has the **determination** to start a task but may lack the ability to always see it through. The thick downstroke shows determination, but the unfinished loop betrays a tendency to go off on tangents, leaving some jobs uncompleted. This is overcome, however, by extreme **persistence,** which we can see in the little "t" crossing "ties." It's almost as if he says to himself: "I'm going to tie it all up!"

One of the most amazing characteristics revealed by his handwriting is intense **optimism** (18). With all the unhappy events in his life at the time of this letter, Ted Kennedy was still able to remain positive in his outlook!

JACQUELINE KENNEDY ONASSIS

Jacqueline Kennedy Onassis, as you know, always appears to be very much in control of herself, and her handwriting shows that she is indeed!

This time I'm going to point out certain traits in the handwriting sample and it's your job to find the strokes that reveal these traits. Ready?

Jacqueline Kennedy Onassis has an **analytical** mind and **loves responsibility.** She listens carefully, learning and remembering what she hears. She has excellent **self-confidence** and is very **intuitive,** sensing or "knowing" when people are sincere with her. There is one thing, however, that is very ironic about this woman: for someone so much in the public eye, she is **sensitive about herself.** She does not like to be talked about, and her feelings are easily hurt.

Not often is she moved by her emotions, though. She is **objective,** letting her mind and intellect rule her emotions (hint, look at the slant of her writing.) This objectivity helps to balance her hypersensitivity. For someone who dislikes being written about, she certainly seems to have chosen the wrong men to marry; on the other hand, her husbands were men who matched the caliber of her own mind. She would have been unhappy with a man less intellectually gifted than she.

From this sample, my impression is of a wise lady with much to offer the world. With her **literary** instincts, it would not be surprising to see her authorship of a book (how interesting to imagine the subject!) This is a special woman who has not received the recognition that she deserves for her own gifts.

MARK TWAIN

The handwriting of **Samuel Clemens**, who was known to most of us **as Mark Twain**, serves as a vivid example of how handwriting changes with the evolution of one's personality.

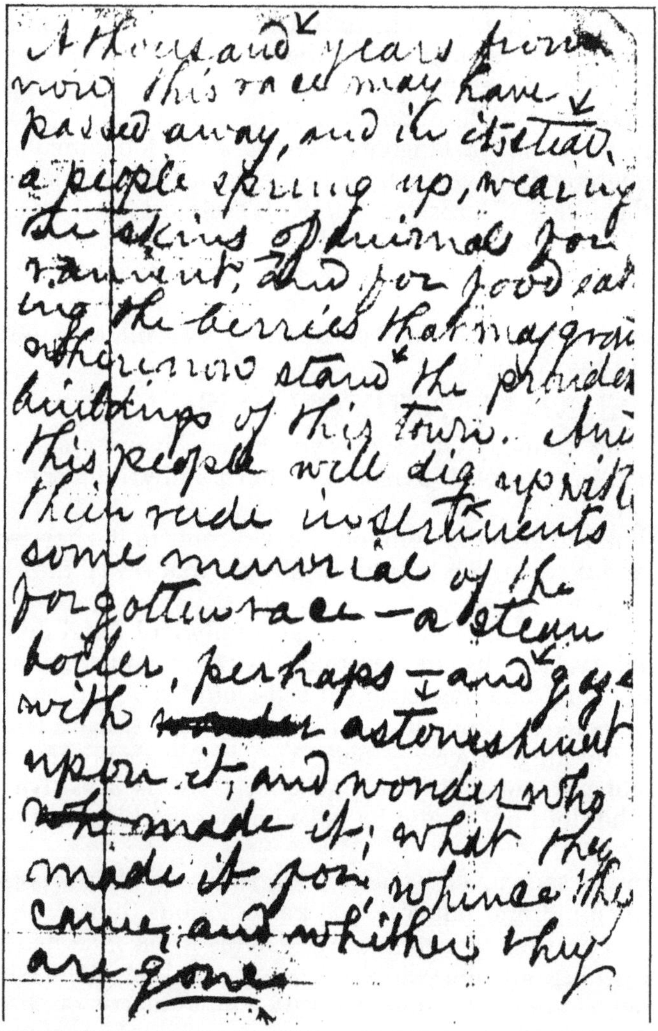
A thousand years from now this race may have passed away, and in their stead a people spring up, wearing the skins of animals for raiment, and for food eating the berries that may grow where now stand the proudest buildings of this town. And this people will dig up with their rude instruments some memorial of the forgotten race—a steam boiler, perhaps—and gaze with ~~wonder~~ astonishment upon it, and wonder who ~~wh~~ made it; what they made it for; whence they came, and whither they are gone.

Fig 20: A page from nineteen-year-old Mark Twain's first notebook.

In a handwriting sample taken from a young Mark Twain's notebook, written when he was 19 we can already see the strong ***literary inclination*** revealed by the "delta d's". Numerous long, sweeping "t" crossings show a tremendous ***enthusiasm,*** and the shorter "t" crossings present in the sample are often very thick, showing excellent ***will power.*** Twain usually dotted his "i's" directly above the stems, indication attention to details. These are all wonderful success-building characteristics for a young writer to possess. Notice, however, that he had not yet developed his ***self-reliance;*** also, the literary "figure 8's" had not yet appeared in his handwriting.

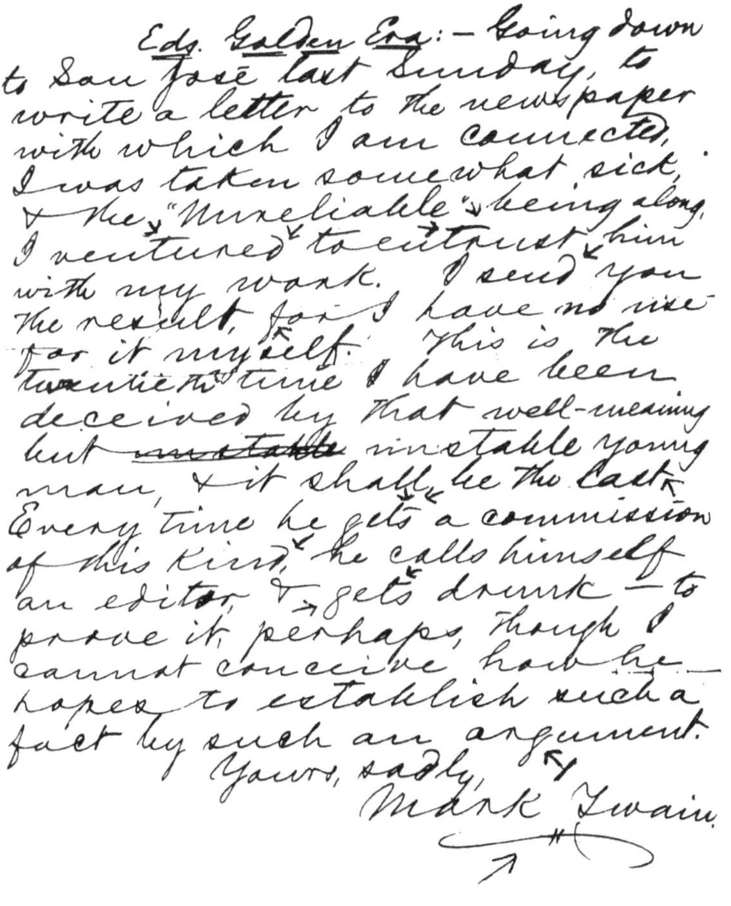

Fig. 21: A letter written by 28-year old Twain to the "Golden Era" literary paper.

In Fig. 21 we can examine the earliest "Mark Twain" signature on record. This handwriting sample is from the year 1863, when Twain was 28 years old. The intervening decade since the previous sample has brought with it some changes in Twain's personality which are reflected in his handwriting.

Notice that the literary "figure 8's" now occur frequently in his writing along with the "delta d's", indicating that Twain's **literary inclinations** were stronger. He has become **self-reliant,** as revealed by the underlined words and the creative flourish beneath his signature. His **self-confidence** is high and his **will power** is still strong. But he shows some **anger** in this sample; see if you can find evidence of it. (Reading the content of the letter shows that he indeed had cause for his anger, or so he believed.)

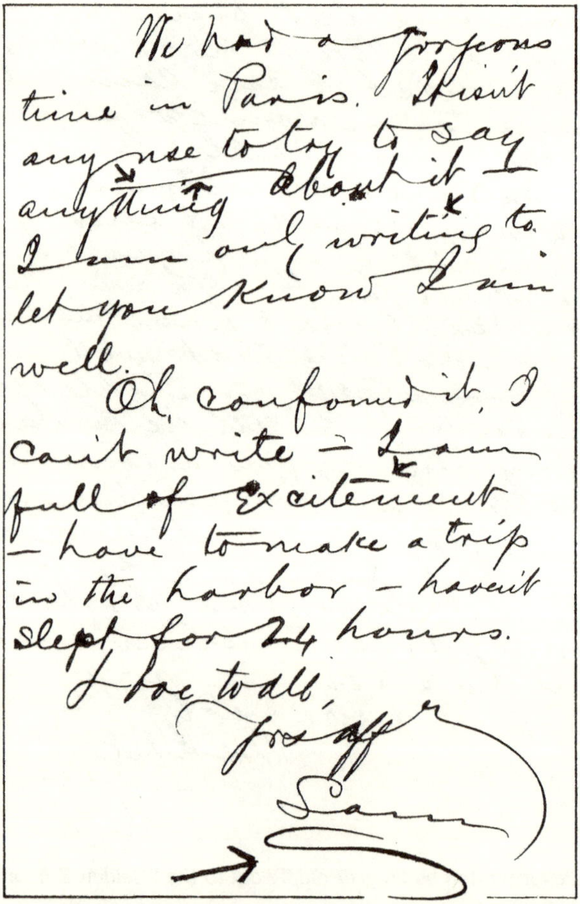

Last page of a letter Mark wrote home from Marseilles on July 12, 1867, reporting on a "gorgeous time" in Paris and so much excitement he couldn't sleep for 24 hours.

Fig 22: A sample of Twain's writing at the age of 32.

When Twain was 32, he wrote a letter home from Marseilles on July 12, 1867, reporting a "gorgeous time" in Paris and so much excitement he couldn't sleep for 24 hours (Fig. 22.) This handwriting sample reflects his tremendous **enthusiasm;** look at the length of the "t" crossing in the word "anything." For some reason we will never know, Twain also shows **anger** in this sample. Perhaps he was angry that his excitement made him unable to write.

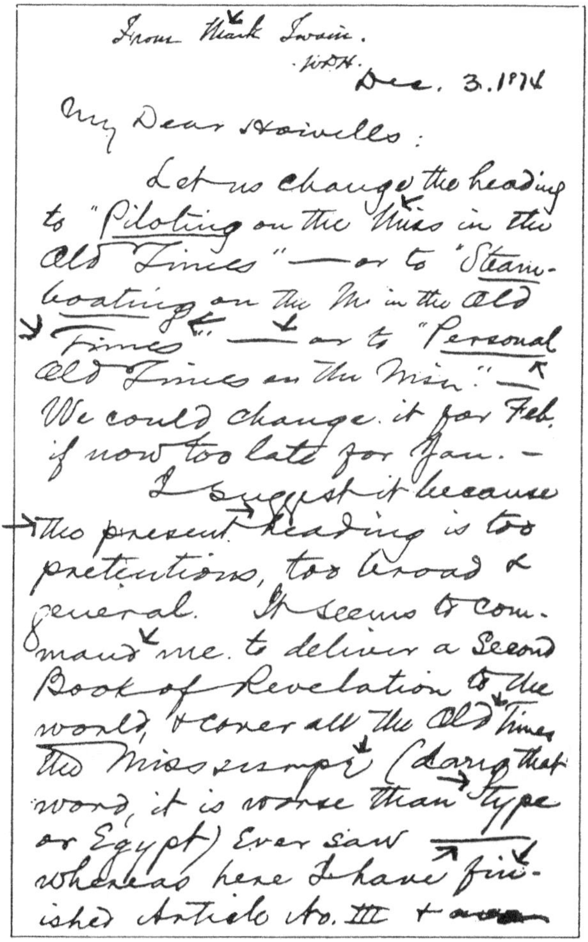

From Mark Twain.
·WDH·
Dec. 3. 1874

My Dear Howells:

Let us change the heading to "Piloting on the Miss in the Old Times" — or to "Steamboating on the M. in the Old Times" — or to "Personal Old Times on the Miss." — We could change it for Feb. if now too late for Jan. —

I suggest it because the present heading is too pretentious, too broad & general. It seems to command me to deliver a Second Book of Revelation to the world, & cover all the Old Time the Mississippi (dang that word, it is worse than Type or Egypt) Ever saw — whereas here I have finished Article No. III & am

Twain writes Howells, editor of the *Atlantic*, to suggest a new title for the magazine series on the Mississippi.

Fig. 23: Nearing 40, Twain wrote this letter to the editor of the Atlantic.

Fig. 23 is a letter that Mark Twain wrote to Mr. Howells, the editor of the *Atlantic,* to suggest a new title for a magazine series on the Mississippi. He was almost 40 years old at the time. The underlining of words shows that Twain had lost none of his ***self-reliance.*** His "m's" and "n's" reveal ***keen comprehension*** to a degree not seen in earlier samples. But this letter also shows ***caution*** — the long, straight dashes — indicating that he wanted to proceed with great care in negotiating the new title for the magazine series. And there is still strong evidence of his ***literary inclinations***: the "delta d's" and "figure 8's". His ***goals*** and ***self-confidence*** remain high.

Elayne V. Lindberg with Gary Lindberg

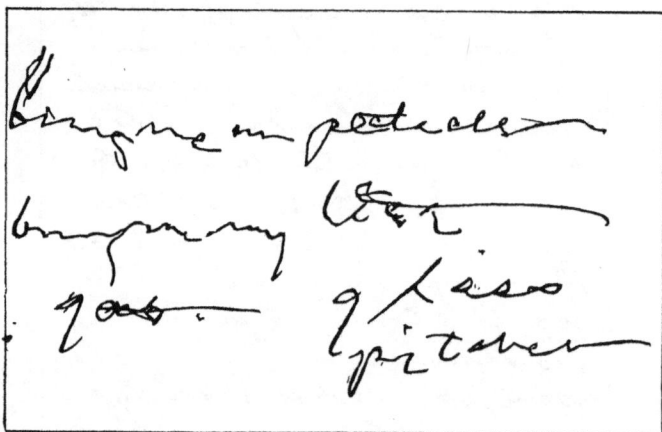

Fig. 24: A handwriting sample from 76-year-old Twain's last day.

In March, 1910, Twain was very ill. Later that month his condition became critical. After one very bad attack of his illness he said, "Well, I had a picturesque night. Every pain I had was on exhibition... I am losing enough sleep to supply a worn-out army." On his last day, he could no longer speak intelligibly. In his last writing (Fig. 24), he requested his spectacles — his glasses — and a pitcher.

This remarkable sample shows a deteriorating mental condition, revealed by handwriting that lacks form compared to previous samples. Amazingly, despite his pain and exhaustion, he was still fighting to remain **enthusiastic.** Mark Twain's last written words provide us with a frighteningly graphic portrait of an ill and dying man.

GEORGE WASHINGTON

While the story of the cherry tree may have been fiction, George Washington's honesty and integrity were fact. And so was his exceptional intelligence.

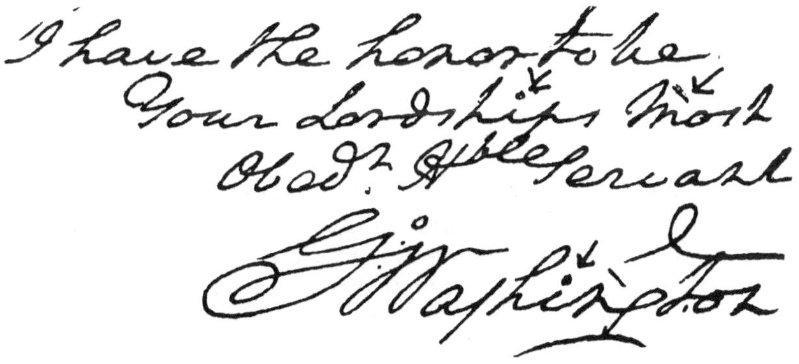

Fig. 25: A younger Washington's handwriting.

See if you can identify the strokes that reveal George Washington's personality. He was, for example, a man of **dignity** and **diplomacy.** At the same time he paid close **attention to details,** he was also **impulsive** (notice the extreme forward slant.)

As a young man, George Washington was a fearless soldier. This fearlessness was enhanced by his impulsiveness and emotional nature (check the slant of the writing.) He didn't always think before he acted. One story claims that two horses were shot out from under him in battle and even though his clothing was riddled with bullet holes, he still pursued the enemy.

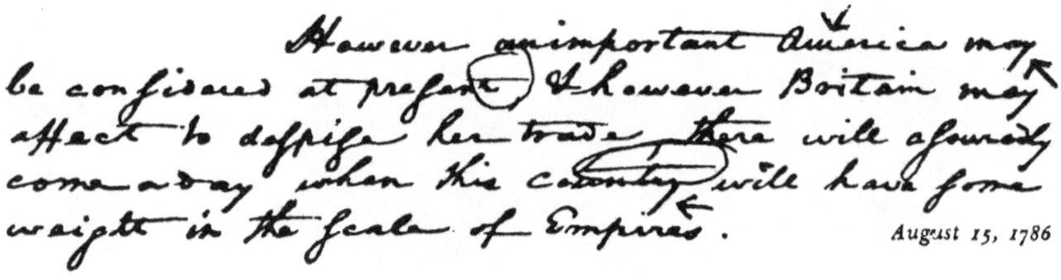

However an important America may be confidered at prefent, & however Britain may affect to defpife her trade, there will afsuredly come a day when this country will have fome waight in the fcale of Empires.

August 15, 1786

Fig. 26: Washington's later handwriting.

Washington frequently forged ahead without too much thought. As he became older, though, he became more **objective** as revealed by the slant of his later handwriting. Whereas the younger Washington's handwriting slanted far to the right, his growing objectivity straightened up the slant in his handwriting as he grew older. Undoubtedly he would not have become the Father of Our Country had he remained so impulsive. Discipline and objectivity are common traits among successful people.

Washington later handwriting shows us other traits, too, that seem to be cornerstones of personal success. **Attention to detail,** good **determination, keen comprehension, loyalty,** and strong **will power.** With age and greater responsibility, Washington's power of **concentration** became greater as well. Concentration is shown by small writing. (**Here is an interesting experiment that uses small writing to test the link between handwriting and your mind.** Take a piece of paper and start to write at the top. Write anything at all, but write much bigger than normal. Large, sweeping strokes. On each subsequent line, make your writing smaller. By the time you reach the bottom of the page your writing should be extremely small and cramped. Now... ask yourself how you feel after reducing your writing down to such tiny strokes. It requires **concentration,** of course, and most people feel "frustrated," "tense," "Oppressed," or "edgy." **Does this tiny writing affect you in this way?)**

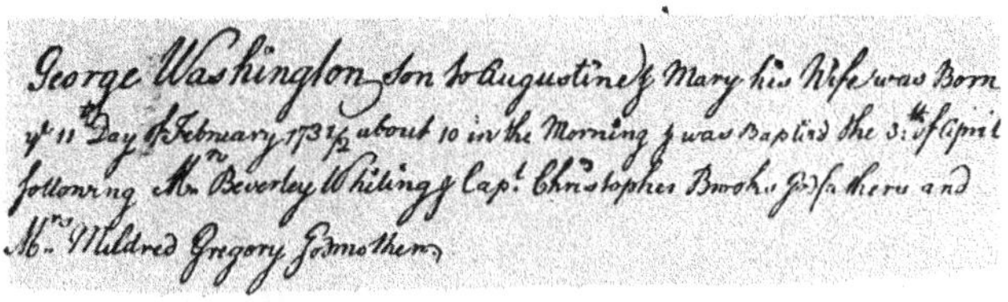
George Washington Son to Augustine & Mary his Wife was Born ye 11th Day of February 1731/2 about 10 in the Morning & was Baptised the 3rd of April following Mr. Beverley Whiting & Capt. Christopher Brooks Godfathers and Mrs. Mildred Gregory Godmother

George's birth record is shown here as it appeared in an old family Bible in his father's handwriting. The inscription states that the boy was born "ye 11th day of February." Twenty years after the record was made the British government ordered the Gregorian calendar, or "new style" as it was called, to be adopted. The deficiency was then eleven days and these were added. Thus, February 22 is now celebrated as Washington's birthday.

Fig. 27: The handwriting of George Washington's father.

Given the written records we have today, it's interesting to speculate on the inheritance of certain traits. Above is a sample of the writing of George Washington's father. you may be able to note similarities in traits between father and son through these samples, most notably ***loyalty*** and ***attention to details.*** But more importantly, do you see similarities between the traits revealed in George Washington's handwriting and your own?

JIMMY DURANTE

Jimmy Durante certainly was different from George Washington. Where George was structured in his thinking, Jimmy was open. Strangely, though, Durante was also quite cautious.

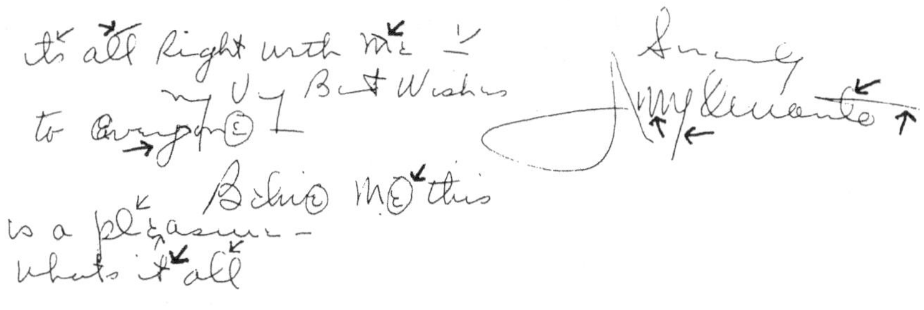

Fig. 28: Jimmy Durante's handwriting.

As a youngster Jimmy was often the target of other kids' jokes about his big nose. His nickname, "The Schnoz," dates back to those early years. Deeply hurt by this insensitivity, he decided even as a child that he would never be guilty of hurting someone else's feelings. In coming to this tough decision, Jimmy became a remarkably ***broadminded*** and compassionate individual. Perhaps this is why millions of people identified with him: he was so vulnerable and human!

Despite his gruff voice and stumbling speech, Durante's handwriting shows a ***literary and cultural appreciation*** one would never have guessed (the "Greek e's".) A large **philosophical imagination** (fat upper zone loops) sharpened by his **analytical mind** (the "v" shape in the middle of many "m's") would have made him interested and concerned about ethical and social matters.

Remember how an "m" with humps that slant down to the right indicates **diplomacy**? The same thing applies to the two "l's" in the word "all" on line three. The second "l" is shorter. This reveals diplomacy... coupled with directness (notice the lack of initial strokes on most words.) Durante could be direct in his speech without hurting anyone's feelings. The second "all" shows a shorter *first* "l", and this indicates **self-consciousness.** I wonder why.

The downstrokes on many lower zone letters shows strong and long-lasting **determination,** and the separation between many letters indicates **intuition.** When Jimmy "felt" something was right, there was no holding him back in pursuing it! His "t" crossings show very **practical goals,** perhaps limited by his self-consciousness. We know he was **sensitive about his work,** too, because the fat loop of the "t" in his signature is wider than the "e" next to it. This reveals sensitivity about oneself, and in a signature usually refers to one's work.

Even in his later years Jimmy held onto his **enthusiasm!** He ran with whatever he felt was right. (Enthusiasm, remember, is revealed by big sweeping "t" crossings. The longer the crossing, the greater the enthusiasm.) Durante also had an extravagant flair in his writing, especially in his signature. A person's *signature,* however, is not the real person; it's only the person that the writer wants you to see!

I wish I had known Jimmy Durante, a person who was much different than the person he projected to the public. My impression is of a brilliant, kind and sensitive man.

BUN AND BURGER

In 1985 I was conducting a weekly call-in show on KMOM, a radio station in Monticello, Minnesota. I know, handwriting analysis on radio sounds like an impossible feat and in the beginning it nearly was. Listeners would call in and describe strokes in their writing and I would attempt some analysis.

Eventually we started to solicit write-ins. Listeners would mail me samples of their handwriting to be analyzed on the air and could use a code name or number to retain anonymity. For me, it produced a bonanza of fascinating samples.

One of the most interesting samples came from two fraternal twins who wondered how similar their personalities were. The twins went by the code names "Bun" and "Burger."

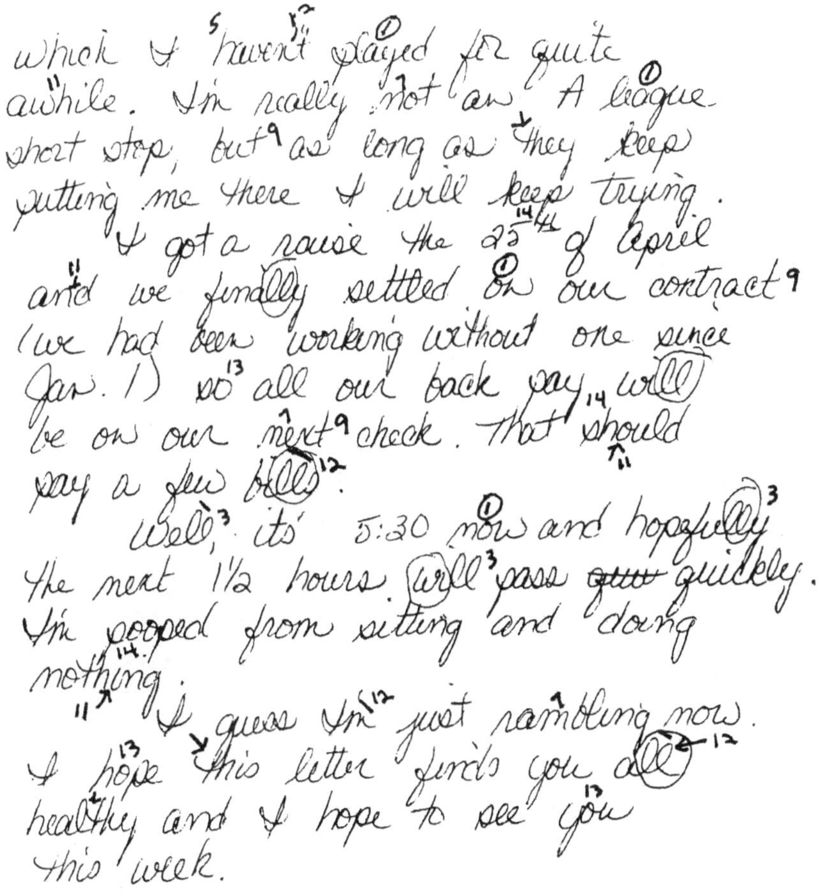

Fig. 29: "Bun's" handwriting sample.

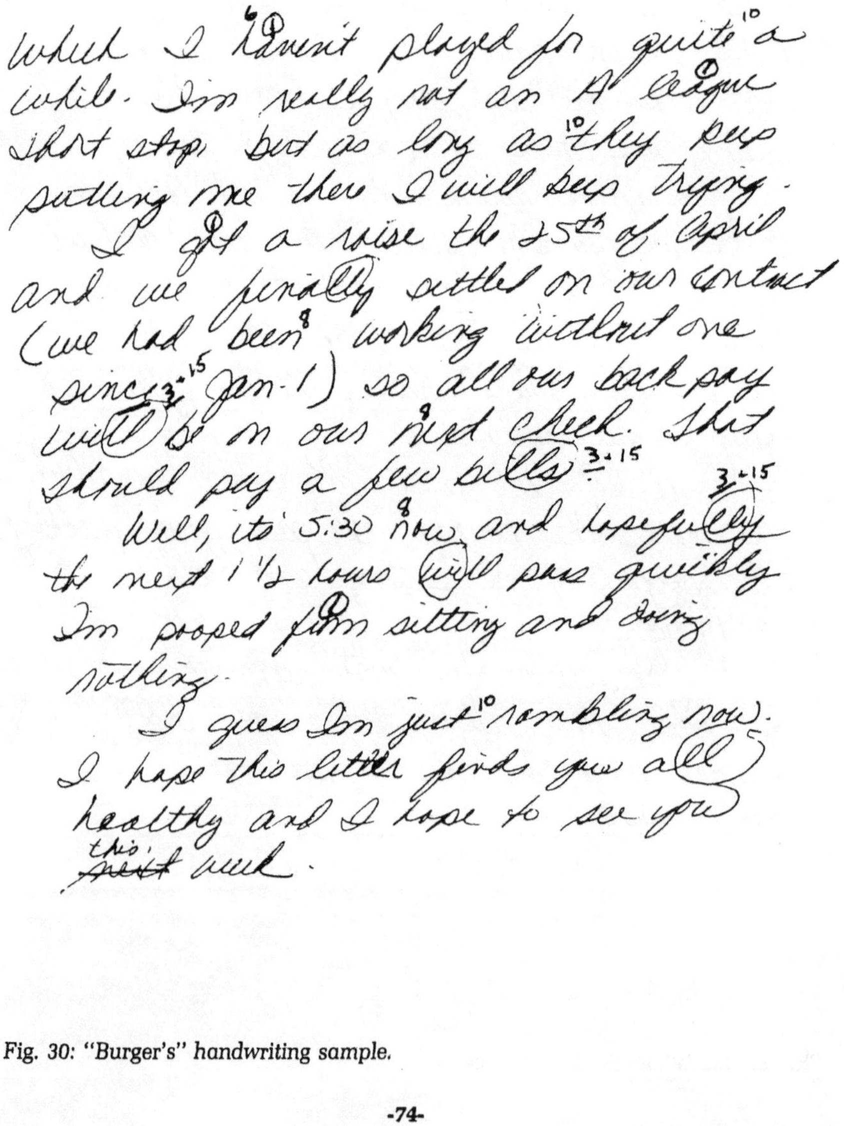

which I haven't played for quite a while. I'm really not an A League short stop but as long as they keep settling me there I will keep trying.

I got a raise the 15th of April and we finally settled on our contract (we had been working without one since Jan. 1) so all our back pay will be on our next check. That should pay a few bills.

Well, it's 5:30 now and hopefully the next 1½ hours will pass quickly. I'm pooped from sitting and doing nothing.

I guess I'm just rambling now. I hope this letter finds you all healthy and I hope to see you next week.

Fig. 30: "Burger's" handwriting sample.

There are some obvious contrasts between these two samples. In Burger's handwriting, for example, the "a's" and "o's" are fat and round. This is the difference between **narrow-minded** and **broad-minded.**

Notice the "double l's" in these samples. Burger's second "l" towers above the first (3): **self-consciousness.** In Bun's version, however, the first "l" is taller than the second (4), indicating tactfulness or **diplomacy.**

Both Bun (5) and Burger (6) place no initial stroke on the word "haven't." We have found a trait they share: **directness.** Either one will tell it like it is. Both of them also exhibit good **manual dexterity** (7 & 8) and **practical goals** (9 & 10.) Manual dexterity shows up in the rounded "m's" and "n". When a "t" crosses in the middle of the stem, it indicates practical goals. (A crossing that looks like a little wash basin, curved up on either end, means the writer is not living up to potential. Burger is living up to her potential; Bun is not.)

Bun has developed her **intuition** (11). She has **diplomacy** (12), knowing you can get most things in life more easily through diplomacy. She's **broadminded** (13), always willing to listen to other people's views. But she has a **"busy mind"** (14) and tends to get involved in thinking about too many things.

Burger is different, more **self-conscious** (15). "Burger, I recommend you stop **procrastinating,**" I told her, hoping she was in my radio audience. "Get on with life! Cross your "t's" all the way through the stem. Forget the past. Move ahead." Listen to people and try to be a little more open-minded."

I finished my quickie analysis and the station switchboard lit up. Here is a transcript of what happened next:

BUN: Hi! This is Bun.

ELAYNE: Hello! How did my analysis sound to you?

BUN: I don't see everything you picked out of my writing, but I saw everything you picked from my twin.

ELAYNE: Interesting, isn't it, that two people born on the same day with the same mother can be so different? Your potential for success is total. You have everything going for you and you know that. You sense that. The one thing that holds your twin back is a little bit of procrastination. Encourage him to go forward and stop thinking about the past.

BUN: I've tried and tried for a long time.

ELAYNE: Just keep trying, okay?

I like to think that Bun kept trying. If anyone could have succeeded, it was Bun.

You may notice that **you** are different from the other members of your family. Though you shared many of the same life experiences, your attitudes toward living may be completely different. Much of this is the result of *how you perceive what happens to you.*

If you write heavily, your experiences are very real and important to you. Bun, for example, writes heavily. She feels deeply, but she reacts to experiences with an open mind. Burger writes heavily, too, but she doesn't listen to other people. She closes her mind before she looks at the total picture.

On the air, I frequently prescribed handwriting excercises for those listeners who wanted to improve in some area. Those who diligently followed the exercises and reported back were rewarded with an in-depth analysis. The incentive produced many case studies regarding the effectiveness of graphotherapy.

The radio analysis were an important step in the development of this book. It became increasingly clear that there were millions of people who were interested in examining and changing their own lives. Only a few of them, unfortunately, were acquainted with the possibilities of graphotherapy.

Now you are among them. you are ready to take a major step in taking charge of your own life and your own personality.

PART III

GRAPHOTHERAPY IN THEORY

The theory behind graphotherapy is simple: **change the handwriting stroke and you change the associated personality trait.**

Graphoanalysis has shown that each stroke in your handwriting means something about you and your personality. If you make a wide upper loop in your "d", it means you are very sensitive. The wider the loop, the more sensitive you are.

Graphotherapy has shown that you can change your behavior — learn to diminish the size of your "d" loop — and consequently become less sensitive. If you remember your goal and practice, the writing exercise consistently for thirty to sixty days, you will notice a distinct change in your life. You will have become less sensitive about yourself.

Graphotherapy is a sound, scientific method of **behavior modification.** It is also one of the **simplest.** Other methods used by psychologists and psychiatrists (bio-feedback, aversion therapy, etc.) involve complicated techniques and in some cases expensive equipment. Graphotherapy requires only pencil and paper.

When you first start changing your normal writing strokes it will feel awkward, like learning a new physical exercise. You may feel a bit uncoordinated for a while. Like any exercise, however, repitition makes it familiar. As with any exercise program, it must become a habit. I want your handwriting exercises to become a habit connected to an actual goal.

This is very important: **the writing exercise must be connected to the desired personality change!** If you have no goal, you will see no change. But when the handwriting modification and the goal become linked, and the exercise becomes habitual, you will gently be reminding yourself each time you write that you WILL achieve your goal. Success will then come automatically.

As one analyst put it: "Handwriting is really *brain-writing*, because the brain controls the muscles of the arm and hand, and the strokes reveal what the brain is telling us." In other words, the simple behavior of writing by hand is inextricably tied to the inner workings of your mind! Change one and you change the other.

In this section I will be giving you the tools to build the positive and productive life that is your birthright. You will learn to retrain yourself, to lose negative habits and establish new positive ones.

This retraining will consist of both mental and physical practice.

For example, if you decide to play the piano you have to train your fingers and your mind at the same time. The same is true of the handwriting exercises you will be starting.

At first the exercises will be mostly physical. They will require a conscious effort. The writing exercises eventually will percolate down into the subconscious. Before long, the mind will accept the new handwriting behavior and integrate it into new patterns being formed in the brain. This is the way to make it work:

1. Find the personality trait you want to work on.
2. Research the handwriting strokes associated with the trait.
3. Practice integrating the new strokes into your handwriting.

There will be a major side benefit of the exercises. I can best describe it with a story about an artist friend of mine. After analyzing his handwriting it became clear that this man was a genius, but there was one thing lacking: self-confidence. He knew that he was a fine artist, but he acknowledged his difficulty in selling himself. He was missing the self-confidence to push ahead in his career.

I started my friend on some handwriting exercises and a month later, at a garage sale, he discovered a small paperback entitled "Pulling Your Own Strings" by Dr. Wayne Dyer. It was a bargain at ten cents, but he told me later that if he had not been doing the handwriting exercises he would have not considered buying the book. The exercises has raised his consciousness so that a book like Dyer's had become important to him. He read the book and was even more inspired to live self-confidently.

The point is this: *if you follow the suggested exercises for thirty days, you will see a change in your personality. New worlds will open up to you.* For a month you will have reinforced your goals hundreds of times and be well on your way to a livelier more successful YOU!

SELF-HELP GOALS

Today every bookstore is overflowing with self-help books. For every human condition there seems to be a fantastic remedy, an exciting plan for change, a new and improved system, a revolutionary discovery.

But let's be realistic, okay?

This book cannot answer everyone's needs. It is, by necessity, a tool box with a terrific set of instructions for building a new you. But you have to do your part. You have to make the decisions and set the goals. You have to do the exercises. You have to tailor it to yourself! The book, in other words, expects you to have certain basic traits to begin with: a degree of determination and the follow-through to complete a task. Without these traits, it's unlikely you will hang in there long enough to see results. As far as the other traits are concerned... let's go to work developing them or getting rid of them!

In the final section of this book we'll assess the important primary traits as they relate to important areas of our lives including: sex, social adaptations, and success.

Sex

I know that some people don't care about sex... or are satisfied completely with their sex lives. But for most of us sex is a powerful motivating force in life. Too often, though, the emphasis in sexual discussion is on "how-to" at the expense of the psychic and social factors. Let us remember that sex does not begin and end below the waist. It begins in the brain, and our personal attitudes and traits determine in a large part how fulfilling our sex lives can be. This is why graphotherapy can be so helpful to the person who has certain kinds of sexual problems.

Graphotherapy will not give you a better body or turn you into the world's greatest lover by Saturday. But it can help you understand the mental side of your sex life and allow you to work on negative traits that may be standing in the way of greater fulfillment.

Social Adaptations

Another common concern is the issue of how we relate to others less intimately — on the social scene. *Social* intercourse often involves a clash of wills, values and intellects.

Many books, from How to Win Friends and Influence People to the more recent Pulling Your Own Strings, state the problem clearly enough, but few offer simple and practical methods for changing behavior for the better. This is where graphotherapy has an edge. We'll look at the traits that affect your social life and you will see clearly your problem areas. Simple, easy exercises will help you change the undesirable traits. You see, graphotherapy not only **identifies the problem but helps you solve it.**

Success

The trouble with talking about success is that everyone has a different definition of it. One person's success is another person's failure. And there's another problem: many so-called successful people seem very unhappy. As **Ben Franklin** once **said,** "Success has ruined many a man."

Too often "success" these days seems interchangeable with notoriety. we admire "successful" people who have done little more than gain a public for what they do. The "successful" author is a best-seller.

I have a different definition: *"success is the happy result of pursuing our highest goals."*

This definition demands, of course, that your success be measured on *your own terms*. The traits necessary for achieving success are the ones that are necessary for you to pursue your highest goals. There is no simpler way of identifying and developing these traits than graphotherapy.

BEGINNING: THE DYNAMIC TRIAD

This is it, step one! A little strategy here will be helpful. Certain traits in certain combinations complement each other in such a way as to make further progress much easier. That's why I strongly suggest this first exercise for *everyone*: THE DYNAMIC TRIAD

SELF-RELIANCE + RAISING GOALS
= GREATER SELF-CONFIDENCE

This is my magic formula. By developing two traits — two strokes in your handwriting — you will achieve an all-important goal of boosting your self-confidence. I don't care how confident you feel, there is always room for improvement.

Here is the exercise in two steps:

1. *Consistently underline your name to improve your self-reliance.*

2. *Raise your "t" crossings by one level to raise your goals.*

FROM   TO

By incorporating these two changes into your handwriting you will automatically boost your self-confidence, the first step in becoming a more dynamic person. The raising of your T crossing indicates higher goals and higher self confidence — **same** stroke means two personality strokes. This exercise is a *must!* But you can go a little further if you like.

One of your new and higher goals should be to increase your self-confidence, which requires you to diligently practice this exercise. The desired change does not occur overnight, but it is guaranteed! Remember the "confidence" stroke is the same as the "higher goals" stroke — a higher "t" crossing — you are tackling your goal in a comprehensive way. On the following page, then, is the DYNAMIC TRIAD EXERCISE.

THE DYNAMIC TRIAD EXERCISE

First, write your name and underline it five times a day for thirty days. Make it a practice to include the underlining **every time you sign your name.**

Secondly, write the word "start". Carefully observe where your "t" bars normally cross the stems and consciously raise the crossing by one level (see UPPER ZONE LETTERS, The Letter "t').

(Write down your first day's exercise here. For the next month use a notebook. At the end of this period check back here and review your progress.)

Williams   *start*

GO SLOWLY WITH THE EXERCISES. DO NOT ATTEMPT TO CHANGE MORE THAN ONE STROKE AT A TIME. I SUGGEST YOU DO THE **DYNAMIC TRIAD** BEFORE ATTEMPTING ANY OTHER EXERCISES.

POWER STROKES AND RED FLAGS

Throughout the remainder of this book we're going to be discussing two basic kinds of primary personality traits as revealed by handwriting strokes. There's a group of good guys and one of bad guys and they live in two opposing camps. One group I call POWER STROKES, and the other group is called RED FLAGS.

The POWER STROKES are found in the handwriting of "can do" people, those who never say never. People who feel confident and experience joy and fulfillment in their lives. POWER STROKES reveal the lively imagination, the self-esteem and loyalty of those go-getters we all admire.

The POWER STROKES are often graphic reminders of a writer's openness and responsiveness to the world. Writers of these strokes are awake and alert, always perceiving what is at the heart of any question. They have high goals pursued with determination, and once they get a handle on a situation, watch out: their persistence and enthusiasm turns them into human dynamos.

RED FLAGS, on the other hand, are found in the handwriting of people whose glass of water is always "half empty" instead of "half full." These are people who seldom lead . They lack the capacity for action prompted by a true feeling of inner confidence.

RED FLAGS need not be feared, however. They represent negative coping skills we have learned in a sometimes unfriendly world. Some of these traits we have learned from parents, others from school. Occasionally a RED FLAG will enter your writing on a temporary basis as a reaction to a recent experience, but all to often these are deeply ingrained traits that stubbornly resist most attempts at taming or elimination.

RED FLAGS are traits that block our success in business, friendships, and other personal and sexual relationships. They keep us from living up to our potential. But there is good news. Since these RED FLAGS are learned, they can be **unlearned!** The quickest and easiest way to retrain the subconscious mind, which controls these traits, is through graphotherapy. And the first step in that process is to identify which traits you possess by completing **THE INSIGHT PERSONALITY PROFILE.**

INTRODUCTION TO
THE INSIGHT PERSONALITY PROFILE

Now it's time for you to find the handwriting sample you wrote earlier. I'm going to guide you through an analysis of your own handwriting, so get ready for some insights. We'll be using a graph called THE INSIGHT PERSONALITY PROFILE which you can find following this introduction.

The PROFILE is divided into three sections. The first section concerns the POWER STROKES in your handwriting: the positive side of the inner you.

The second section of the PROFILE is called RED FLAGS and is a list of the possible negative traits you may have acquired during your lifetime. These are "warning signals" at a railroad crossing: Stop — Look — Listen.

The third section will help you identify the kind of THINKING PROCESSES that dominate your mind. The way we think, of course, has a great bearing on all the other traits.

Through writing exercises, your POWER STROKES can be strengthened and your RED FLAGS eliminated. Your success in accomplishing such feats, however, depends entirely on your dedication and persistence in following the instructions TO THE "LETTER."

Immediately following THE INSIGHT PERSONALITY PROFILE chart is a complete set of instructions to guide you stroke by stroke through an analysis of your handwriting. The strokes you identify will be logged onto the PROFILE chart for use later.

THE INSIGHT PERSONALITY PROFILE

POWER STROKES

		1	2	3	4	5	6	7	8	9	10	11	12	13	14	15	16	17	18	19	20	21
1	SELF-RELIANCE																					
2	GOOD GOALS																					
3	GOOD CONFIDENCE																					
4	ATTENTION TO DETAILS																					
5	KEEN COMPREHENSION																					
6	WILL POWER																					
7	ENTHUSIASM																					
8	INITIATIVE																					
9	ORGANIZING ABILITY																					
10	PHILOSOPHICAL IMAGIN																					
	MATERIAL IMAGINATION																					
11	DECISIVENESS																					
12	DETERMINATION																					
13	PERSISTENCE																					
14	DIPLOMACY																					
15	EXPLORATORY THINKING																					
16	OPTIMISM																					
17	TALKATIVENESS																					
18	SENSE OF HUMOR																					
19	BROADMINDED																					
20	LOYALTY																					
21	MANUAL DEXTERITY																					
22	GENEROSITY																					
23	GOOD SELF-CONTROL																					
24	LOVES PHYS ACTIVITY																					
25	INTUITIVE THINKING																					
26	LOGICAL THINKING																					
27	GOOD COLOR SENSE																					
28	INDEPENDENT THINKING																					
29	LITERARY INCLINATION																					
30	PURSUE ARTISTIC AREA																					

My name is Bill Benson and I have self-reliance. In this case I will have total triumph tomorrow which requires total attention to true self-confidence. I need to initiate higher attention to details. I find that my writing shows a comprehending mind. Thick "t" crossings stands for strong will which helps me become totally enthusiastic. It is time to start right and act right. The gift of organization often fashions fame. I'm flying high in my big imagination. To exercise is not an easy decision. The "lower case" letter "3" shows my unyielding quality Why do you fall every season — turn, turn, turn. Is it because all men and women matter? The physical people perchance persist and perhaps proud proper people who are physical people put pride in their profession. So prepare your papers in the proper position.

Bill Benson

123a

THE INSIGHT PERSONALITY PROFILE

POWER STROKES

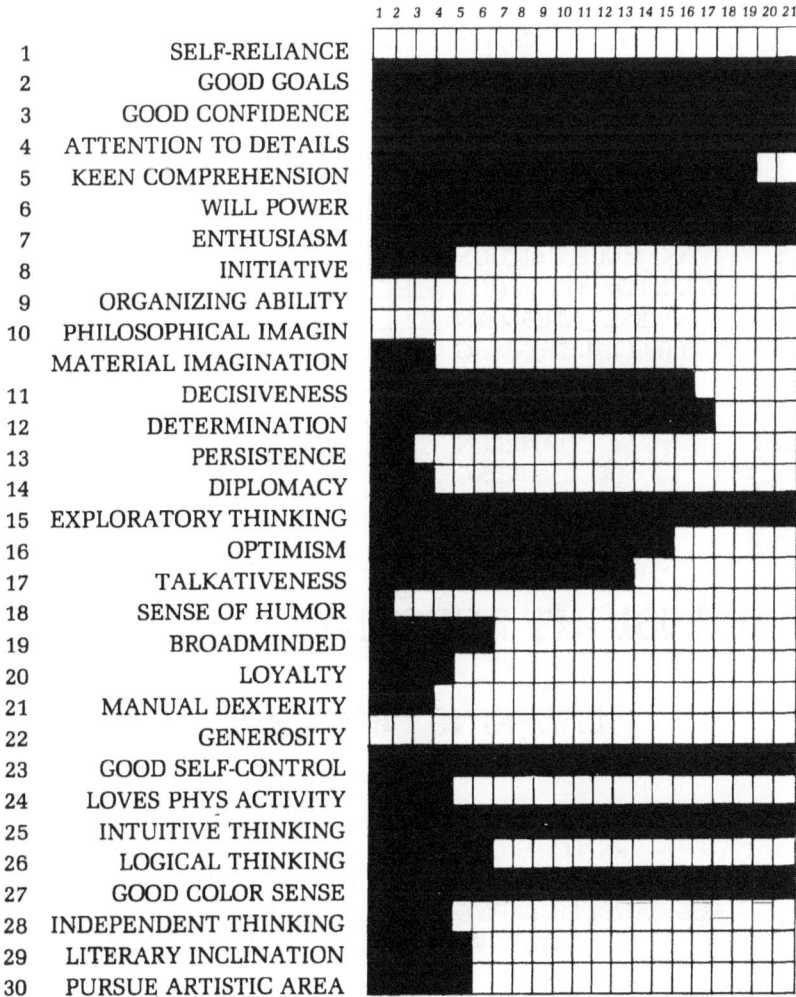

		1 2 3 4 5 6 7 8 9 10 11 12 13 14 15 16 17 18 19 20 21
1	SELF-RELIANCE	
2	GOOD GOALS	
3	GOOD CONFIDENCE	
4	ATTENTION TO DETAILS	
5	KEEN COMPREHENSION	
6	WILL POWER	
7	ENTHUSIASM	
8	INITIATIVE	
9	ORGANIZING ABILITY	
10	PHILOSOPHICAL IMAGIN	
	MATERIAL IMAGINATION	
11	DECISIVENESS	
12	DETERMINATION	
13	PERSISTENCE	
14	DIPLOMACY	
15	EXPLORATORY THINKING	
16	OPTIMISM	
17	TALKATIVENESS	
18	SENSE OF HUMOR	
19	BROADMINDED	
20	LOYALTY	
21	MANUAL DEXTERITY	
22	GENEROSITY	
23	GOOD SELF-CONTROL	
24	LOVES PHYS ACTIVITY	
25	INTUITIVE THINKING	
26	LOGICAL THINKING	
27	GOOD COLOR SENSE	
28	INDEPENDENT THINKING	
29	LITERARY INCLINATION	
30	PURSUE ARTISTIC AREA	

Bill Benson's Graph

THE INSIGHT PERSONALITY PROFILE

RED FLAGS

		1	2	3	4	5	6	7	8	9	10	11	12	13	14	15	16	17	18	19	20	21
1	OVERLY SENSITIVE																					
2	RESENTMENT																					
3	SELF-CONSCIOUS																					
4	PROCRASTINATION																					
5	TEMPER																					
6	SELF-CASTIGATION																					
7	JEALOUSY																					
8	TOO MUCH CAUTION																					
9	DESIRE FOR ATTENTION																					
10	OVERLY STUBBORN																					
11	SUPERFICIAL THINKING																					
12	SHALLOW THINKING																					
13	REPRESSION																					
14	CONFUSION																					
15	DOMINEERING																					

THE INSIGHT PERSONALITY PROFILE

THINKING PROCESSES

1	ANALYTICAL
2	EXPLORATORY
3	KEEN COMPREHENSION
4	LOGICAL/CUMULATIVE
5	INTUITIVE

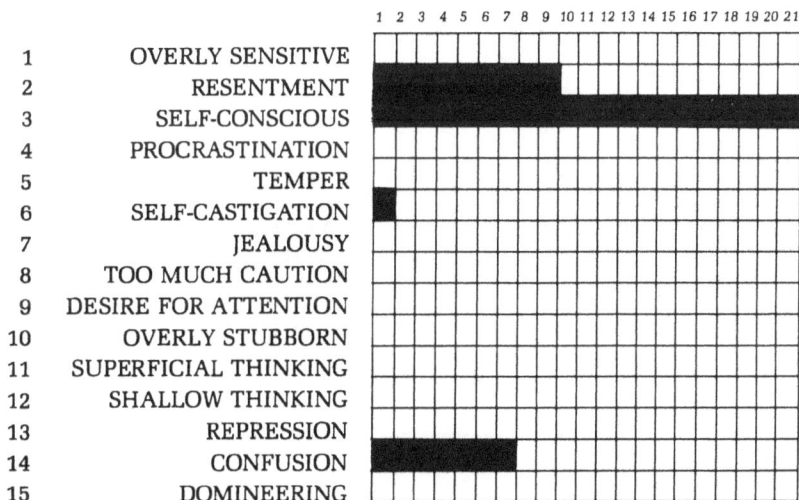

THE INSIGHT PERSONALITY PROFILE

RED FLAGS

		1 2 3 4 5 6 7 8 9 10 11 12 13 14 15 16 17 18 19 20 21
1	OVERLY SENSITIVE	
2	RESENTMENT	
3	SELF-CONSCIOUS	
4	PROCRASTINATION	
5	TEMPER	
6	SELF-CASTIGATION	
7	JEALOUSY	
8	TOO MUCH CAUTION	
9	DESIRE FOR ATTENTION	
10	OVERLY STUBBORN	
11	SUPERFICIAL THINKING	
12	SHALLOW THINKING	
13	REPRESSION	
14	CONFUSION	
15	DOMINEERING	

THE INSIGHT PERSONALITY PROFILE

THINKING PROCESSES

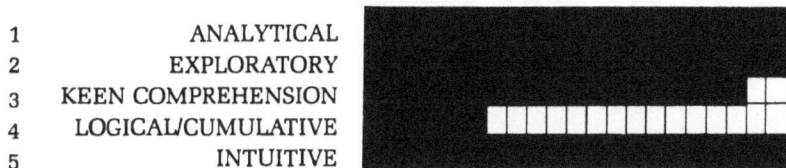

1	ANALYTICAL
2	EXPLORATORY
3	KEEN COMPREHENSION
4	LOGICAL/CUMULATIVE
5	INTUITIVE

Bill Benson's Graph

INSTRUCTIONS FOR COMPLETING YOUR INSIGHT PERSONALITY PROFILE

THE SEARCH FOR POWER STROKES

SELF-RELIANCE

1.) Search your handwriting sample for **SELF-RELIANCE.** This is indicated by underlining your name or a word in a sentence. There are three types of underlines that qualify, including a single underline going from left to right, and a creative flourish.

EXAMPLES:

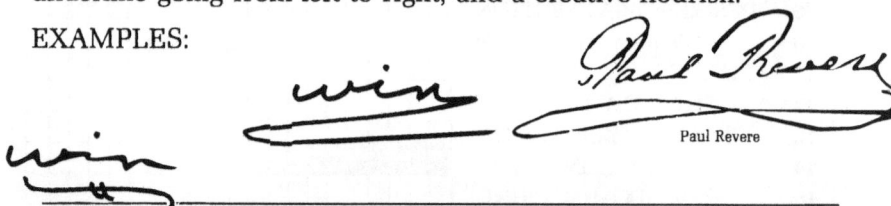

Paul Revere

(Single underline and creative flourish.)

The third type of underlining to qualify is a *double* underline, but only when made in this specific way: the stroke must begin by going from right to left, then abruptly reverse itself to go in the other direction. Below are two examples, one which indicates self-reliance (RIGHT) and one which does not (WRONG).

EXAMPLES:

RIGHT: WRONG:

(Double underline)

Each time you see this POWER STROKE in your handwriting sample, fill in one box in ROW 1: SELF-RELIANCE.

GOOD GOALS

2.) Search your handwriting sample for **GOOD GOALS** (Practical or High.) This is shown by where you cross your "t's". For purposes of this profile, the "t" crossings must fall between lines 3 and 4 as shown below.

Florence Nightingale

(Use plastic guide #3)

Use your plastic graph guide to measure your "t" crossings. Guide #3 contains five groups of lines labelled A-F. One of these groups should match the height of the "t" stem you are measuring. If it fits, the top line of the guide will rest on the top of the "t" stem as the bottom line creates a base line for your "t".

Note: Your "t" stems may vary in height, so use the group of lines that best fits each stem "to a t." And MEASURE ACCURATELY!

(If the *greater percentage* of your crossings are *above* the "t" stem, you are exhibiting excessive daydreaming. I suggest you practice lowering some of your crossings until they touch the top of the stems. This will help bring some of your flights of fancy back to reality.)

Each time you see this POWER STROKE in your handwriting sample, fill in one box in ROW 2: GOOD GOALS.

GOOD CONFIDENCE

3.) Search your handwriting sample for **GOOD CONFIDENCE**. This also involves your "t" crossings. Good self-confidence is indicated whenever the crossing is on line 3 or higher (see previous trait, GOOD GOALS, for proper measuring technique.)

EXAMPLES:

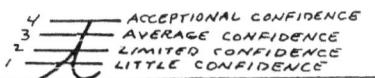

Francis Scott Key, Writer of Star Spangled Banner.

(A "t" crossing of 3 or higher.)

"Wait a minute!" you say. "I just checked that." And you did. The stroke that reveals high self-confidence also indicates good goals. This means that one graphotherapy exercise can change two **traits!** This fact is the basis for my magic formula called THE DYNAMIC TRIAD:

SELF-RELIANCE + RAISING GOALS

= GREATER SELF-CONFIDENCE

Many of us have talked ourselves into thinking we have self-confidence, but our "t's" are tattle-tales.

Each time you see this POWER STROKE in your handwriting sample, fill in one box in ROW 3: GOOD CONFIDENCE

ATTENTION TO DETAILS

4.) Search your handwriting sample for **ATTENTION TO DETAILS.** This is indicated by the dotting of the "i" and "j". To count as attention to details, the dot must be directly over the stem of the letter.

EXAMPLES:

Dwight D. Eisenhower

(The dot is directly over the stem.)

Each time you see this POWER STROKE in your handwriting sample, fill in one box in ROW 4: ATTENTION TO DETAILS.

KEEN COMPREHENSION

5.) Search your handwriting sample for **KEEN COMPREHENSION.** This is revealed by sharp, needlepoint strokes on the top of "r", "m", "n", and "h".

EXAMPLES:

Harry Houdini

(Sharp "needlepoint" strokes.)

Each time you see this POWER STROKE in your handwriting sample, fill in one box in ROW 5:" KEEN COMPREHENSION.

WILL POWER

6.) Search your handwriting sample for **WILL POWER**. For this trait, again check your "t" crossings. If they are short and thick in comparison to your other writing, it counts as will power.

EXAMPLES:

Mozart

(Thick, short "t" crossings.)

Each time you see this POWER STROKE in your handwriting sample, fill in one box in ROW 6: WILL POWER.

ENTHUSIASM

7.) Search your handwriting sample for **ENTHUSIASM**. Look for long "t" crossings! If the length of the crossing is greater than the height of the T stem it counts as enthusiasm the longer the stroke, the greater the enthusiasm. For an accurate measurement, use Guide #3.

EXAMPLES:

Sincerely, yours

Harry S. Truman, 33rd president of the U.

("t" crossing longer than the stem.)

Each time you see this POWER STROKE IN YOUR HAND-WRITING SAMPLE, FILL IN ONE BOX IN ROW 7: EN-THUSIASM.

INITIATIVE

8.) Search your handwriting sample for **INITIATIVE**. Look for any "r", "h", or "t" that is the last letter of a word. A final stroke that leaves the baseline and pushes outward, as below, can be counted as initiative.

EXAMPLES:

William H. Taft, 27th President of the U.S.

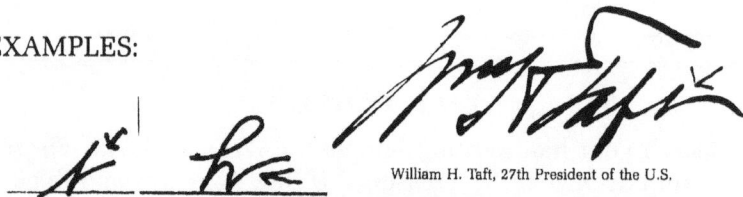

(The final stroke pushes outward.)

Each time you see this POWER STROKE in your handwriting sample, fill in one box in ROW 8: INITIATIVE.

ORGANIZATIONAL ABILITY

9.) Search your handwriting sample for **ORGANIZATIONAL ABILITY,** also known as "balance in thinking." The upper and lower lower loops in the "f" should be identical in size. If there are no loops, the top and bottom strokes must be the same length.

EXAMPLES:

George Washington

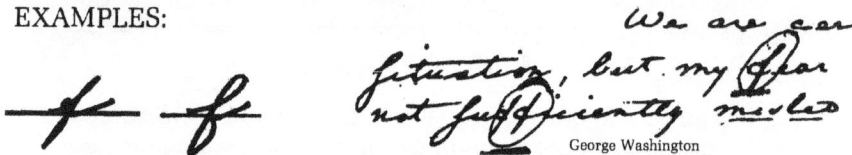

(Same size upper and lower loops.)

Each time you see this POWER STROKE in your handwriting sample, fill in one box in ROW 9: ORGANIZING ABILITY.

IMAGINATION

10.) Search your handwriting sample first for **PHILOSOPHICAL IMAGINATION.** In the upper zone letters "b", "h", "k" and "l", the loops must be between 1 and 1½ times the width of companion middle zone letters to be counted as above average. Use Guide #3 for accurate measurement.

EXAMPLES:

Henry Longfellow (even if writing is small)

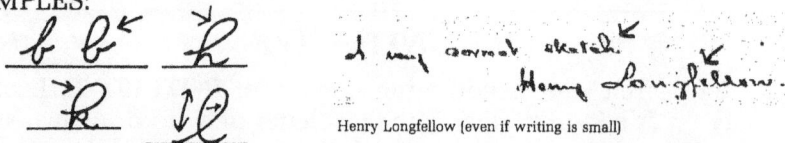

(Lower loops 1 to 1½ times the width of middle zone letters.)

Each time you see this POWER STROKE in your handwriting sample, fill in one box in ROW 10: PHILOSOPHICAL IMAGINA-TION.

Now search your handwriting for **MATERIAL IMAGINATION.** Look at the lower loops in the letters "g", "y", "q" and "z". To count as above average material imagination, these loops must be between 1 and 1½ times the width of companion middle zone letters. Use Guide #3 for accurate measurement.

EXAMPLES:

Groucho Marx

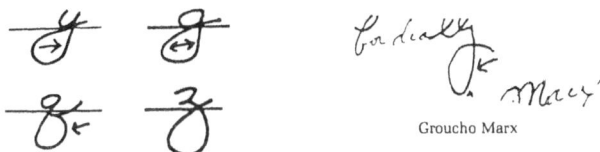

(Lower loops 1 to 1½ times the width of middle zone letters.)

Fill in boxes in ROW 10: MATERIAL IMAGINATION.

DECISIVENESS

11.) Search your handwriting sample for **DECISIVENESS.** Look for any blunt end strokes, or an increase in weight at the end of any final stroke in a word.

EXAMPLES:

1799   George Washington

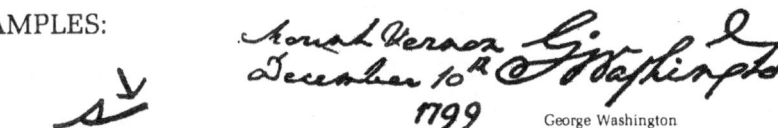

(Blunt ends on final strokes.)

Each time you see this POWER STROKE in your handwriting sample, fill in one box in ROW 11: DECISIVENESS.

DETERMINATION

12.) Search your handwriting sample for **DETERMINATION.** The relative heaviness or thickness of the downstroke in lower zone letters indicates good determination, a firm intention *to do* what needs to be done. The relative length of the stroke show for how long the writer will be determined, and the heaviness shows the strength of that determination. These strokes must be judged in comparison with other strokes in your writing sample.

EXAMPLES:

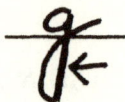
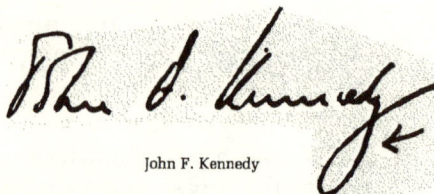

John F. Kennedy

(Note thickness and length of downstrokes.)

Each time you see this POWER STROKE in your handwriting sample, fill in one box in ROW 12: DETERMINATION.

PERSISTENCE

13.) Search your handwriting sample for **PERSISTENCE**. Look for the "tie" stroke in the "t", "q", "f", "y" or any other letter. This little knot-like configuration counts as persistence.

EXAMPLES:

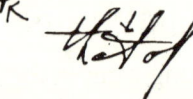

RIGHT: Mrs. Nolan, Aunt of Harry Truman   WRONG:

(The "tie" stroke.)

Each time you see this POWER STROKE in your handwriting sample, fill in one box in ROW 13: PERSISTENCE.

DIPLOMACY

14.) Search your handwriting sample for **DIPLOMACY**. Carefully check each "m", "n", "ll" and "tt". The tops of these letters — or double-letters — must slant downward to the right before they can count as diplomacy.

EXAMPLES:

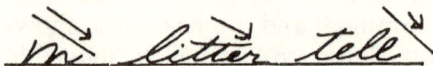
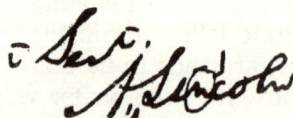

A. Lincoln

(A downward slant to the right.)

Each time you see this POWER STROKE in your handwriting sample, fill in one box in ROW 14: DIPLOMACY.

EXPLORATORY THINKING

15.) Search your handwriting sample for **EXPLORATORY THINKING,** or CURIOSITY. Look at the letters "m", "n", "h" and "r". Do they have a "tent-like" look to them? If they look like upside-down "v's", they count. Think of these sharp peaks as mountain tops the explorer sets out to conquer.

EXAMPLES:

Heinrich Himmler, Hitler Chief of Staff

(The "mountain tops" of exploratory thinking.)

Each time you see this POWER STROKE in your handwriting, fill in one box in ROW 15: EXPLORATORY THINKING.

OPTIMISM

16.) Search your handwriting sample for **OPTIMISM.** The optimism stroke is identified by an upward slant to the "t" crossing, as shown below. Also, this trait can be shown by words that have an upward thrust within the sentence context.

EXAMPLES:

account of my invention

show Light

Yours T

Thomas Edison

(Optimism means "looking up.")

Each time you see this POWER STROKE in your handwriting sample, fill in one box in ROW 16: OPTIMISM.

TALKATIVENESS

17.) Search your handwriting sample for **TALKATIVENESS**. Look for the letters "a" and "o" that are open on the top.

EXAMPLES:

Madonna

(An open circle stroke, like an open mouth, shows talkativeness.)

Each time you see this POWER STROKE in your handwriting sample, fill in one box in ROW 17: TALKATIVENESS.

SENSE OF HUMOR

18.) Search your handwriting sample for a **SENSE OF HUMOR**. Look for "m", "n", "w" and "y". These letters sometimes have a small curve or flair in the initial stroke that indicates sense of humor.

EXAMPLES:

Mamie Doud Eisenhower, wife of 34th president of the U.S.

(A curve or flair in the initial stroke.)

Each time you see this POWER STROKE in your handwriting sample, fill in one box in ROW 18: SENSE OF HUMOR.

BROADMINDED

19.) Search your handwriting sample for **BROAD-MINDEDNESS**. Look for the round letters "a", "e", "o", "d" and "s". If they are well-rounded, they count as broadminded.

EXAMPLES:

(Open circles, open minds.)

Each time you see this POWER STROKE in your handwriting sample, fill in one box in ROW 19: BROADMINDED.

LOYALTY

20.) Search your handwriting sample for **LOYALTY**. Look for round, firm dots on the "i" and "j".

EXAMPLES:

Miles Standish

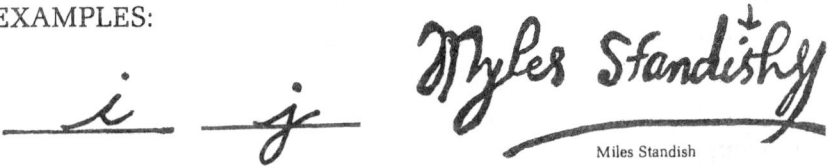

(Round, firm dots.)

Each time you see this POWER STROKE in your handwriting sample, fill in one box in ROW 20: LOYALTY.

MANUAL DEXTERITY

21.) Search your handwriting sample for **MANUAL DEXTERI-TY**. This trait is indicated by rounded tops on the "m" and "n", and by a flat top on the "r".

EXAMPLES:

Helen Keller

(Round tops, but a flat "r".)

Each time you see this POWER STROKE in your handwriting sample, fill in one box in ROW 21: MANUAL DEXTERITY.

GENEROSITY

22.) Search your handwriting sample for **GENEROUS** nature. Look for final strokes on words. When a final stroke "reaches out" for a distance at least equal to the width of the preceding letter and then turns **up**, it counts as a generosity stroke.

EXAMPLES:

Clark Gable

("Reaching out" the width of a preceding letter.)

Each time you see this POWER STROKE in your handwriting sample, fill in one box in ROW 22: GENEROSITY.

GOOD SELF-CONTROL

23.) Search your handwriting sample for **GOOD SELF-CONTROL.** Try to find "t" crossings that are bent to look like upside down bowls. *The more bend to the crossing, the more intense is the self-control.*

EXAMPLES:

Abraham Lincoln

(The upside down bowl.)

Each time you see this POWER STROKE in your handwriting sample, fill in one box in ROW 23: GOOD SELF-CONTROL.

LOVES PHYSICAL ACTIVITY

24.) Search your handwriting sample for an indication that you **LOVE PHYSICAL EXERCISE.** The letter'p" provides it. The bigger the lower loop, the greater the tendency toward physical activity. This may only indicate a tendency to watch sports or other activities, but the tendency exists when this stroke is present.

EXAMPLES:

Humphrey Bogart

(A big lower loop stands for "physical.")

Each time you see this POWER STROKE in your handwriting sample, fill in one box in ROW 24: LOVES PHYSICAL EXERCISE.

INTUITIVE THINKING

25.) Search your handwriting sample for **INTUITIVE THINK-ING**. Look for breaks or interruptions of letters within words.

EXAMPLES:

Martha Jefferson

(A separation of some letters within words.)

Each time you see this POWER STROKE in your handwriting sample, fill in one box in ROW 25: INTUITIVE THINKING.

LOGICAL THINKING

26.) Search your handwriting sample for **LOGICAL THINKING**. Here, you will look for the same strokes as "Manual Dexterity:" rounded tops on the "m" and "n" and a flat-top "r". If you wish, copy the chart from row 21 onto row 26.

EXAMPLES:

Eva Peron

(The same strokes as "Manual Dexterity.")
Each time you see this POWER STROKE in your handwriting sample, fill in one box in ROW 26: LOGICAL THINKING.

GOOD COLOR SENSE

27.) Search your handwriting sample for a **GOOD COLOR SENSE**. This is shown not by a stroke, but by *heavy* pressure on the writing instrument. The heavier the writing, the more color awareness you have.

EXAMPLES:

heavy   *light*   *Wyatt D. Earp.* ←

Wyatt Earp

(Heavy pressure shows color awareness.)

If you see this POWER STROKE in your handwriting sample, fill in boxes in ROW 27: GOOD COLOR SENSE. For medium pressure, fill in half the boxes, etc.

INDEPENDENT THINKING

28.) Search your handwriting sample for **INDEPENDENT THINKING**. Look for the letters "d" and "t'. If the stems of these letters are the same height as the middle zone letters, or shorter, independent thinking is indicated.

EXAMPLES:

d

toad

Joan Crawford

(Short stems = independent thinking.)

Each time you see this POWER STROKE in your handwriting sample, fill in one box in ROW 28: INDEPENDENT THINKING.

LITERARY INCLINATION

29.) Search your handwriting sample for **LITERARY INCLINA-TION**. Look for the letters "g", "y" and "q" which contain loops that look like the number "8'. Also look for any "e" that is written like a "Greek E" or capital E.

EXAMPLES:

Francis Scott Key

Edgar Allan Poe

P.T. Barnum

(Figure 8's and Greek E's.)

Each time you see this POWER STROKE in your handwriting sample, fill in one box in ROW 29: LITERARY INCLINATION.

PURSUE ARTISTIC AREA

30.) Search your handwriting sample for a desire to **PURSUE ARTISTIC AREAS**. The indicator strokes are the same as those of "Literary Inclination." If you wish, you may copy the chart for Row 29 onto Row 30.

EXAMPLES:

(These are the same strokes as Literary Inclination.)

INSTRUCTIONS FOR COMPLETING YOUR INSIGHT PERSONALITY PROFILE

THE SEARCH FOR RED FLAGS

OVERLY SENSITIVE

1.) Search your handwriting sample for an **OVERLY SENSITIVE** nature. Look for "d's" with large upper loops. To count, the loop must be between 1 and 1½ times the width of the nearest "e" or "a". The wider the "d" loop, the more sensitive the writer in the areas of *dress and personality.*

EXAMPLES:

(A loop wider than the nearest "e" or "a".)

Each time you see this RED FLAG in your handwriting sample, fill in one box in ROW 1: OVERLY SENSITIVE.

RESENTMENT

2.) Search your handwriting sample for **RESENTMENT.** Look for a straight, inflexible initial stroke that begins a word. This straight stroke can be attached to any letter.

EXAMPLES:

(A straight initial stroke on any letter.)

Each time you see this RED FLAG in your handwriting sample, fill in one box in ROW 2: RESENTMENT.

SELF-CONSCIOUS

3.) Search your handwriting sample for **SELF-CONSCIOUS**. This trait is indicated by strokes in the letters "m", "n", "ll" and "tt". These strokes must slope down to the left as shown.

EXAMPLES:

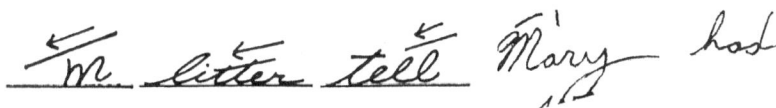

(A visible slope to the left.)

Each time you see this RED FLAG in your handwriting sample, fill in one box in ROW 3: SELF-CONSCIOUS.

PROCRASTINATION

4.) Search your handwriting sample for **PROCRASTINATION**. Look for the crossings of the "t". When a cross-bar starts to the left of the stem but does not cross it, count the stroke as procrastination.

EXAMPLES:

(A "t" crossing that doesn't catch up with the stem.)

Each time you see this RED FLAG in your handwriting sample, fill in one box in ROW 4: PROCRASTINATION.

TEMPER

5.) Search your handwriting sample for **TEMPER**. Look for the short, straight, little "temper tick" at the beginning of a word.

EXAMPLES:

left Walton's Mountain, with a body

(The "temper tick".)

Each time you see this RED FLAG in your handwriting sample, fill in one box in ROW 5: TEMPER.

SELF CASTIGATION

6.) Search your handwriting sample for **SELF-CASTIGATION**. This is indicated by a final stroke that reverses itself over the last letter.

EXAMPLES:

give *have not met at this time*

(A final stroke that shifts into reverse.)

Each time you see this RED FLAG in your handwriting sample, fill in one box in ROW 6: SELF-CASTIGATION.

JEALOUSY

7.) Search your handwriting sample for **JEALOUSY**. Look for small, flattened loops in the beginning or initial strokes of the letters "m", "n", "y", "w" and "t".

EXAMPLES:

y w t m *Thanks Much*

(Jealousy loops in the initial stroke.)

Each time you see this RED FLAG in your handwriting sample, fill in one box in ROW 7: JEALOUSY.

TOO MUCH CAUTION

8.) Search your handwriting sample for **TOO MUCH CAUTION**. Try to find **long**, straight final strokes at the end of words, or straight dashes at the end of lines.

EXAMPLES:

(Cautious endings.)

Each time you see this RED FLAG in your handwriting sample, fill in one box in ROW 8: TOO MUCH CAUTION.

DESIRE FOR ATTENTION

9.) Search your handwriting sample for **DESIRE FOR ATTEN-TION**. Look for circles that dot the the the "i's".

EXAMPLES:

(Circles over your "i's".)

Each time you see this RED FLAG in your handwriting sample, fill in one box in ROW 9: DESIRE FOR ATTENTION.

OVERLY STUBBORN

10.) Search your handwriting sample for an **OVERLY STUB-BORN** nature. Look for "t's" that form short "tent-like" figures.

EXAMPLES:

(The stubborn tent-like "t".)

Each time you see this RED FLAG in your handwriting sample, fill in one box in ROW 10: OVERLY STUBBORN

SUPERFICIAL THINKING

11.) Search your handwriting sample for **SUPERFICIAL THINK-ING.** Look for any loose, unformed, soft strokes such as those shown.

EXAMPLES:

(Loose, unformed strokes.)

Each time you see this RED FLAG in your handwriting sample, fill in one box in ROW 11: SUPERFICIAL THINKING.

SHALLOW THINKING

12.) Search your handwriting sample for **SHALLOW THINK-ING.** Look for any bowl-shaped "t" crossings.

EXAMPLES:

(The bowl-shaped crossing.)

Each time you see this RED FLAG in your handwriting sample, fill in one box in ROW 12: SHALLOW THINKING.

REPRESSION

13.) Search your handwriting sample for **REPRESSION.** This is indicated by an *upward retracing* of a downstroke in the letters "m", "n" and "h". If a majority of these candidate strokes contain such retracing, it means you are repressing something.

EXAMPLES:

m   *snot*   *met*

(Uward retracing of a downstroke.)

Each time you see this RED FLAG in your handwriting sample, fill in one box in ROW 13: REPRESSION.

CONFUSION OF INTERESTS

14.) Search your handwriting sample for a **CONFUSION OF INTERESTS.** Look for writing that contains upper or lower loops overlapping the line of writing above or beneath it it. Each overlapping stroke counts one.

EXAMPLES:

(Confused writing, confused interests.)

Each time you see this RED FLAG in your handwriting sample, fill in one box in ROW 14: CONFUSION.

DOMINEERING

15.) Search your handwriting sample for a **DOMINEERING PRESENCE.** Look for "t" crossings that slant down to the right and become thinner, like an arrow pointing.

EXAMPLES:

(The "domineering" arrow pointed at the ground.)

Each time you see this RED FLAG in your handwriting sample, fill in one box in ROW 15: DOMINEERING.

INSTRUCTIONS FOR COMPLETING YOUR INSIGHT PERSONALITY PROFILE

THE SEARCH FOR THINKING PROCESSES

ANALYTICAL

1.) Search your handwriting sample for *ANALYTICAL THINK-ING*. Look for the "v" shape inside such letters as "m", "n", "r", "w" and sometimes even the "u".

EXAMPLES:

(A "v" hidden inside other letters.)

Each time you see this THINKING PROCESS in your handwriting sample, fill in one box in ROW 1: ANALYTICAL.

EXPLORATORY

2.) Search your handwriting sample for *EXPLORATORY THINKING*. This is the same as 15 on the POWER TRAITS chart. If you wish, you may simply copy that row here. If you'd rather practice some more, here is a review.

Look at the letters "m", "n", "h", "w", "l", "p" and "r". Do they have a "tent-like" look to them? If they look like upside-down "v's", they count. Think of these sharp peaks as mountain tops the explorer sets out to conquer.

EXAMPLES:

(The "mountain tops" of exploratory thinking.)

Each time you see this THINKING PROCESS in your handwriting sample, fill in one box in ROW 2: EXPLORATORY.

KEEN COMPREHENSION

3.) Search your handwriting sample for **KEEN COMPREHENSION**. This is the same as 5 on the POWER TRAITS chart. If you wish, you may simply copy that row here. If you'd rather practice some more, here is a review.

Keen Comprehension is revealed by sharp, needlepoint strokes on the top of "r", "m", "n" and "h".

EXAMPLES:

(Sharp "needlepoint" strokes.)

Each time you see this THINKING PROCESS in your handwriting sample, fill in one box in ROW 3: KEEN COMPREHENSION.

LOGICAL THINKING

4.) Search your handwriting sample for **LOGICAL THINKING**. This is the same as 26 on the POWER TRAITS chart. If you wish, you may simply copy that row here. If you'd rather practice some more, here is a review.

Logical thinking (and manual dexterity, you will recall) are identified by rounded tops on the "m" and "n" and a flat-top "r".

EXAMPLES:

forced to write right.

m n r

(The same strokes as "Manual Dexterity".)

Each time you see this THINKING PROCESS in your handwriting sample, fill in one box in ROW 4: LOGICAL / CUMULATIVE.

INTUITIVE THINKING

5.) Search your handwriting sample for **INTUITIVE THINKING**. This is the same as 25 on the POWER TRAITS chart. If you wish, you may simply copy that row here. If you'd rather practice some more, here is a review. Look for breaks or interruptions of letters within words.

EXAMPLES: *used to judge the hand*

Sep ar ation

(A separation of some letters within words.)

Each time you see this THINKING PROCESS in your handwriting sample, fill in one box in ROW 5: INTUITIVE.

INTRODUCTION TO
THE EXERCISES

The completed INSIGHT PERSONALITY PROFILE chart gives you a graphic look at your relative strengths and weaknesses. Take time to study it. Undoubtedly you will find that much of it rings true. The appearance of certain traits in your personality, however — or the absence of some — may surprise you. This is quite normal. Even though we think we know ourselves well, there is always something more to learn.

Remember, if you have accurately measured and properly identified the strokes, this PROFILE will be an amazingly accurate portrait of your personality **on the day** you wrote your handwriting sample.

Now it is time to take your personality into your own hands ... literally! Through simple graphotherapy exercises you can enhance your strengths, acquire new POWER TRAITS, eliminate unwanted RED FLAGS, hone your thinking processes and reshape a more confident, more dynamic YOU!

Before proceeding with additional exercises, you must complete the DYNAMIC TRIAD exercise assigned earlier. I know you're probably eager to plunge ahead, but please take things in the proper order. You should never attempt to change more than one stroke at a time (except in the DYNAMIC TRIAD exercise.) It has taken you years to assemble the traits that comprise your personality today; you cannot successfully attempt a major overhaul all at once. Take each trait individually and work on it. When you have succeeded in changing that stroke — and its associated trait — then move on.

This one-at-a-time approach is not original. A few years ago, a man named **Benjamin Franklin concocted this same scheme for personal improvement.** He was concerned about some of his own negative traits and bad habits, so he set out to change. He began by compiling a list of those virtues he believed were necessary for success, virtues he wanted to acquire or nurture. His list was as follows:

1. Temperance
2. Silence
3. Balance (Mental)
4. Resolution
5. Prudence

6. Industry
7. Sincerity
8. Justice
9. Moderation
10. Cleanliness
11. Tranquility
12. Humility

Working on all these virtues at once would have required more of his attention than he could spare, so he vowed to tackle each in turn, one-at-a-time. As an aid, he created a journal in which each virtue was allotted a page. Like an accountant, he kept score of his progress and his occasional regressions. he worked diligently on each virtue until he was satisfied that he had acquired it absolutely.

Did it work for the great man? At the age of 79 he wrote an autobiography in which he spent more time discussing this practice than anything else, crediting much of his success and happiness to it. He wrote, "I hope, therefore, that some of my descendents will follow the example and reap the benefits."

Sound advice, indeed. It can work for you, too. Study your PROFILE and make a priority list of those traits you want to acquire, eliminate or improve. In the following section you will find a more detailed discussion of each trait and a simple but effective graphotherapy exercise that can help to change your life! The traits in this section are numbered the same as in the INSIGHT PERSONALITY PROFILE.

Have fun and ... write on!

THE POWER TRAITS AND GRAPHOTHERAPY EXERCISES

1. SELF RELIANCE

Self-reliance is the first of human qualities
because it guarantees all others.

W. Fields

Wise words. So much of life requires us to rely on our own resources and function independently. **If you are a self-reliant person, you instinctively take things into your own hands. You are personally responsible for your own actions.** When a job needs to be done, you forge ahead and do it without depending on anyone or anything.

At first glance it may seem that self-reliance would interfere with a mature, adult sexual relationship, but this is not true. Self-reliance is not narcissism or unhealthy egotism; it is a strength of character that ultimately is very sexy.

Think of it this way: others perceive you as you perceive yourself. You project to others the person you perceive yourself to be. if you see yourself as unlovable, you will be seen by others as unlovable. The self-reliant person, however, feels worthy of another's trust, respect and love. When you trust yourself, others trust you. if you respect and love yourself, you become lovable to others.

In social life the same is true. We have all been in a social situation with someone who has a magnetic personality. These kinds of people have a special sense of themselves and seem to operate at the center of some greater power. These are strong, self-reliant personalities who, rather than pushing others away, draw everyone to them. **Self-reliance is an essential trait in dealing with the world in day-to-day relationships.**

Self-reliance is shown in handwriting by the underlining of

words in a text, ***especially your signature.*** This makes sense, doesn't it? By underlining a signature the writer seems to be saying, "This is me, and don't you forget it!" The underscore is a graphic affirmation of the individual.

Fig. 31: Underlining of words or phrases (especially your signature) = self-reliance.

Following is a collection of signatures from famous people. Each one shows the trait of self-reliance by adding an underscore or creative flourish beneath the signature.

Signature samples from the collection of the artist, Bill Mack.

Most scholarly of the Presidents; kept interminable diary. When he broke his
made entries with left hand. Served in Congress after Presidency.

Andrew Jackson (1829-1837)

1. *Napoleon I, emperor of France.
The creamy pastry bears his name.*

James K. Polk (1845-1849)

AN EXERCISE FOR SELF-RELIANCE

Write: "Self-reliance" and your own signature five times a day for thirty days. Be sure to underline each phrase and signature as you complete it. Also, whenever you sign your name — to a letter, a memo, a check, etc. — try to remember to underline your signature.

Write out your first day's exercise here. For the next month write your exercises in a notebook acquired for this use alone. After one month, check back here and evaluate your progress.

_____

_____

_____

_____

_____

self-reliance   Bill Benson

As you write your exercises, it is important to think about what self-reliance means. As you begin, the exercise may feel a bit awkward and artificial. As you make progress, however, you will notice how automatic the underlining becomes. Once the stroke is habit, it has become linked in your mind with the behavior. Then each time you underline a phrase or signature you will be reinforcing your self-reliance.

2. GOALS

*The goal stands up, the keeper
stands up to keep the goal.*

A. E. Houseman

Your goals are your intentions: what you intend to do today, tomorrow, next week, next month, next year. Goals are the focus of your attention. The clearer your focus, and the clearer your idea of what you want to accomplish, the more apt you are to achieve your goal.

Your goals may be low or high. A high goal like "getting a college education" usually involves many smaller, lower goals, such as accumulating funds for one semester. This, of course, would only be one of the goals that must be met before the high goal of "college education' is realized.

To obtain your high goals, it is a good practice to set simple, realistic, stepping stone goals that can be more easily accomplished in a short time span. Meeting goals, no matter how small, raises your confidence bit by bit so that the higher long-range goals seem more attainable.

Our goals in life are so intimately linked to our image of ourselves (see SELF-CONFIDENCE) that it is hard to discuss one without the other. High goals and self-confidence are closely tied together because a positive self-image is the result of accomplishment. When we achieve our own goals, we feel good about ourselves. No one is so lovable as someone who is able to love himself.

Without goals, without something to shoot for, there can be little direction in life and no sense of accomplishment. The writer with high goals and self-confidence, however, has a sense of mission that helps create a dynamic personality: a person with a clear direction and the belief that he's got what it takes to get there.

It is possible, of course, to have too many goals that are too high, too visionary. We must be realistic or we'll spend all our time daydreaming about the distant future instead of accomplishing achievable goals in the near term.

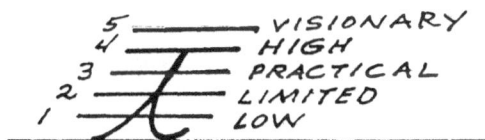

Fig. 33: The level of the "t" stem indicates the relative level of goals: (1) Low; (2) Limited; (3) Practical; (4) High (5) Visionary.

(1) LOW GOALS. If you exhibit primarily low goals in your handwriting, you are finding it difficult to accept yourself as you are. You probably find yourself looking with envy at the success of others while you ignore your own potential.

(2) LIMITED GOALS. If most of your "t" crossing strokes reveal limited goals, it means that you are easily satisfied — perhaps too easily. Most likely you have a poor opinion of your abilities and lack confidence in the worthiness of your actions.

(3) PRACTICAL GOALS. These are average, every-day goals that reach no higher than necessary. If you show mainly practical goals in your sample, you are a person who wants to be sure of success, telling yourself, "Don't set the goals too high! You may not achieve them." You are not giving full challenge to your capabilities.

(4) HIGH GOALS. This is an indication of a dynamic, exciting personality. If your "t" strokes show this level of goals predominantly, you have set for yourself challenging performance standards. You keep striving for improvement and are willing to risk failure to see how far you can go. You want to give full challenge to your abilities. (As you can see, without high self-confidence no one would establish high goals.)

(5) VISIONARY GOALS. An occasional "visionary goal" in your handwriting can be an exciting find. Once in a while, when your "t" crossing soars *above* the stem itself, it means that you are daring to dream! What a wonderful quality to have. *If most of your crossings are above the stem, however, it shows persistent and fruitless daydreaming with little attempt to bring goals down to reality.*

AN EXERCISE FOR ADJUSTING GOALS

If you are comfortable with your goals in life, skip this exercise. Most people, however, can benefit by boosting their goals just a bit. (A few people need to lower them.) This exercise requires you to reposition your "t" crossings on the stem.

Write; *"Total triumph tomorrow;"* five times per day for thirty days. Watch where you usually cross your "t's". Consciously raise your crossing by *one level*, but no higher than the top of the stem. (If you normally cross your "t's" above the stem, then *lower* your crossing until it intersects the stem itself.)

Write out your first day's exercise here. For the next month write your exercises in a notebook acquired for this use alone. After one month, check back here and evaluate your progress.

_____

_____

_____

_____

_____

total triumph tomorrow

This is an exercise to help you to change your attitude toward your goals in life. As you cross your "t's" in this exercise, consciously remind yourself that you are adjusting your goals with each stroke. *Beyond this exercise, consciously adjust your "t" crossings whenever you write.*

3. SELF CONFIDENCE

So much is a man's worth, as he
has confidence in himself.

Rabelais

Even the instinctively self-reliant person (previously discussed) cannot amount to much without faith in his own powers and judgment. **Self-confidence insures that we will not become paralyzed into inaction.**

My research has shown that most people lack true self-confidence. You see, true self-confidence is not just boasting. It is genuine faith in one's personal capabilities. It is a rational, objective assessment of oneself based on experience and free of irrational doubt.

Most of us underestimate our capabilities even though our self-confidence takes a beating in the process. Those of us who judge ourselves too harshly can easily raise the levels of our self-confidence without risk of achieving a boastful extreme.

Self-confidence is necessary to a rewarding sex life, too. Without it, no one would initiate a relationship. A lack of self-confidence is a self-imposed sentence to a life of passivity and even impotence.

Self-confidence is also sexy. Think about this the next time someone catches your eye. What was it that attracts you? Chances are it will be more than an arrangement of facial features or the style of clothes. It probably will be the way it all somehow comes together in that person: the walk, the poise, the look of inner "something". Self-confidence shows! The confident person is immediately alluring, even from a distance. this trait has made more favorable first impressions than any other.

When you have high self-confidence you feel worthwhile, you trust yourself, you have confidence in your abilities. Handwriting samples from great people inevitably reveal this trait.

Establishing self-confidence is **one** of the first steps toward personal success. It is revealed in handwriting by the same stroke that indicates goal levels: the "t" crossing.

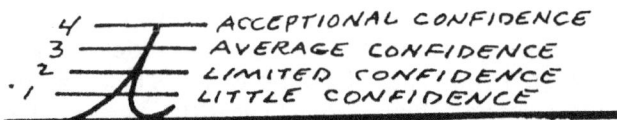

Fig. 34: The height of the "t" crossing tells the level of self-confidence: (1) Excellent; (2) Good; (3) Limited; (4) Low.

AN EXERCISE FOR ADJUSTING SELF-CONFIDENCE

If you are comfortable with your self-confidence, skip this exercise. Most people, however, can benefit by boosting their self-confidence just a bit. This exercise requires you to reposition your "t" crossings on the stem.

Write: *"Total attention to true self-confidence"* five times per day for thirty days. Watch where you usually cross your "t's". Consciously raise your crossing by *one* level, but no higher than the top of the stem. (If you normally cross your "t's" above the stem, then *lower* your crossing until it intersects the stem itself.)

Write out your first day's exercise here. For the next month write your exercises in a notebook acquired for this use alone. After one month, check back here and evaluate your progress.

_____

_____

_____

_____

_____

Total attention to true self-confidence

This is an exercise to help you improve your self-confidence. As you cross your "t's" in this exercise, consciously remind yourself that you are working on developing confidence. *Beyond this exercise, consciously adjust your "t" crossings whenever you write.*

Lift t's crossing

EXAMPLE

4. ATTENTION TO DETAILS

"Attention to details" describes a person with a sharp eye and the ability to confer meaning to the smaller things in life. Remember the song, "The Little Things Mean A Lot?"

As any relationship becomes more intimate, little details take on much greater significance. A couple, for example, can come to know each other so well that even the smallest details can pull them together or force them apart. Couples who are close often have little private jokes, secret signals, favorite gestures or special understandings that require a subtle but detailed knowledge of each other's life. Attention to these positive details can be the cement that holds a relationship together even after romantic passion has cooled.

On the other hand, in every relationship there are little habits on both sides that drive the other person crazy. Paying attention to these little things mean a lot, too.

Sometimes the details are physical, as in sex. Physical love is more action than words, but a person who pays close attention to the tiniest details of lovemaking is a more responsive, more generous lover.

In social situations, little things distinguish us as thoughtful friends: remembering names, anniversaries, birthdays; the ability to catch small details of conversation, both spoken and unspoken (body language, facial expression, special signals, etc.) The person who does not pay attention to such details risks appearing insensitive and detached.

In the early stages of any creative endeavor, knowing, appreciating and keeping track of the details helps guarantee the success of the effort. **We win battles by winning skirmishes.**

Minute events are the hinges on which magnificent events turn.

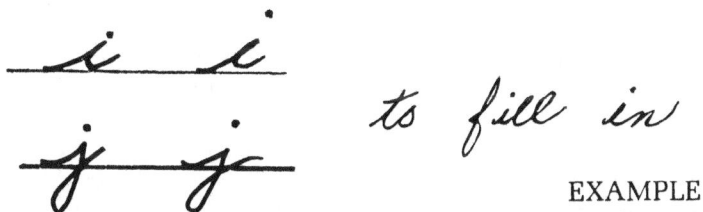

EXAMPLE

Fig.35: Attention to details is revealed by a dot placed directly over an "i" or "j".

AN EXERCISE FOR ATTENTION TO DETAILS

Write: **'initiate higher attention to details''** five times per day for thirty days. Pay special attention to the "i" dot, making sure it is placed directly above the stem of the letter.

Write out your first day's exercise here. For the next month write your exercises in a notebook acquired for this use alone. After one month, check back here and evaluate your progress.

This is an exercise to help you pay more attention to the details of life. As you dot your "i's" in this exercise, consciously remind yourself that you are learning to pay attention to details with each stroke. *Beyond this exercise, consciously adjust your "i" dots whenever you write.*

5. KEEN COMPREHENSION

What a man doesn't understand,
He doesn't have.

Goethe

Keen comprehension is the ability to understand ideas and situations *quickly*. The word "comprehension" literally means to "grasp mentally." The keenly comprehensive mind "understands" concepts and processes almost before they have been revealed. Sometimes understanding comes so quickly it almost makes one want to cry out, "Eureka!" (Occasionally this leads to frustration, when understanding comes well before the end of a painfully long explanation.)

The "World's Best Lovers" are always those who are most responsive to their partners, understanding their needs. Keen comprehension allows a lover to pick up and understand even the tiniest signals from a partner. This creates an almost psychic sense of "knowing" what the other person wants.

Can you walk into a party and size up the room at a glance. With a party of good friends, it's a cinch. You know their moods and behaviors so well, if something is amiss you can catch it right off. But if you have a keenly comprehensive mind, you can catch the same subtle signals in a roomful of strangers. You can understand the social pecking order almost immediately and know who is angry or standoffish. You'd be less likely to make the kind of social faux pas we all fear.

Keen comprehension also makes you a good conversationalist. You are seldom at a loss for words because you quickly see to the heart of a conversation and join in appropriately. You immediately understand what others are saying, or trying to say, and sometimes you can even help them explain their points.

The ability to discover quickly the heart of a problem makes this trait almost indispensable for the person in business, the artist, the journalist... the Mom! Success is usually the culmination of a long series of problems solved in a timely fashion. If you can grasp things quickly, you can achieve your goals that much sooner. The keenly comprehensive mind wastes no time on the road to success.

As you've probably guessed, KEEN COMPREHENSION AND ATTENTION TO DETAILS go hand in hand. They enhance each other. "Details" are the input to the computer in your head; "comprehension" is knowing what to do with them.

Fig. 36: Keen comprehension is shown by sharp, "needlepoint" strokes.

AN EXERCISE TO INCREASE COMPREHENSION

Write: **"my writing shows a comprehending mind"** five times per day for thirty days. Work hard on creating or developing the sharp "needlepoint" strokes on the tops of the letters "h", "m", "n", "r" and "w".

Write out your first day's exercise here. For the next month write your exercises in a notebook acquired for this use alone. After one month, check back here and evaluate your progress.

_____

_____

_____

_____

This is an exercise to help you increase your comprehension. As you sharpen your "needlepoint" strokes in this exercise, consciously remind yourself that you are developing your powers of comprehension with each stroke. _Beyond this exercise, consciously adjust your strokes in these middle zone letters each time you write._

EXAMPLE

6. WILL POWER

...that which we are, we are;
One equal temper of heroic hearts,
made weak by time and fate, but strong in will
to strive, to seek, to find
and not to yield.

Alfred Lord Tennyson (Ulysses)

Will power is directly related to the strength with which we set our goals. The will is defined as "the faculty by which the mind makes conscious, deliberate choices." **When the will takes over, reasoning ends and uncertainty is over: a choice has been made.**

When that crossing is *short* and *thicker* than most other writing strokes, you are exhibiting a strong will.

If you are strong-willed, you will not hesitate to make necessary choices and take action. **A strong will gives you the strength to overcome obstacles and accomplish your purpose in life.**

First you must have the will to take action; then the action taken helps you as an individual. *When we will, we act; when we act, we create our selves.*

Fig. 37: *Will power is shown by short, thick "t" crossings (made heavier than other strokes.)*

AN EXERCISE FOR WILL POWER

Write: **"thick t crosses stand for strong will"** five times per day for thirty days. Consciously make your "t" crossings short and thick relative to the other strokes in your handwriting.

Write out your first day's exercise here. For the next month write your exercises in a notebook acquired for this use alone. After one month, check back here and evaluate your progress.

_____

_____

_____

_____

_____

thick t crossings stand for strong will.

This is an exercise to help you increase your will power. As you cross your "t's" in this exercise, consciously remind yourself that you are improving your will power with each stroke. *Beyond this exercise, consciously make short, thick "t" crossings whenever you write.*

EXAMPLE   *Day 14*

to details today

7. ENTHUSIASM

*Nothing great was ever achieved
without enthusiasm.*

Ralph Waldo Emerson

Enthusiasm is intense or eager interest. A fervor. A poetic ecstasy. It is revealed in handwriting by long, sweeping crossings of the "t".

In the sexual area, enthusiasm is an eager devotion to or fondness for someone. Enthusiasm adds snap and crackle to every happy relationship, increasing the warmth and intensity of passion.

Enthusiasm puts a magnifying glass over many other traits, enhancing them or making them stronger, higher, more intense.

It's sad that youthful enthusiasm sometimes fades, and with it the zeal with which life has been lived. Capturing — or recapturing — a measure of enthusiasm can make a person sexier and more dynamic at any age.

In social situations enthusiasm can set a personality apart from the crowd — in a most positive sense. Most people are attracted to enthusiasm, perhaps because they feel the need for more of it and they know that it's contagious. Our enthusiasm can be directed toward specific areas of interest, and in so doing we tend to attract friends and acquaintances who share our enthusiasms.

Successful people commonly show an abundance of enthusiasm in their handwriting.

Fig. 38: Long, sweeping "t" crossings are an indication of enthusiasm.

AN EXERCISE TO ACHIEVE GREATER ENTHUSIASM

Note: The "t" is an important letter in graphotherapy. It is involved in other important traits, too, such as self-confidence and will power. Check out these other traits and, as you practice this exercise, keep them in mind. You could end up with higher goals, more self-confidence and increased enthusiasm! All thanks to the letter "t".

Write: *"totally enthusiastic"* five times per day for thirty days. Concentrate on making the "t" crossings long and sweeping, at least longer than the "t" stems themselves.

Write out your first day's exercise here. For the next month write your exercises in a notebook acquired for this use alone. After one month, check back here and evaluate your progress.

_____

_____

_____

_____

_____

totally enthusiastic

This is an exercise to help you increase your enthusiasm. As you cross your "t's" in this exercise, consciously remind yourself that you are growing more enthusiastic with each stroke. *Beyond this exercise, consciously lengthen your "t" crossings whenever you write.*

EXAMPLE *t then returns*

8. INITIATIVE

Well begun is half done.

Horace

The word "initiative" comes from a Latin word that means "beginning." Initiative is not only the power to take the first step, but also the power to take the next step in any endeavor.

Without this power we are inert. Without the power to begin we can never finish. This is the essence of success: you must be able to take the first step.

Initiative is shown in our handwriting by a strong stroke that breaks away from the baseline. This "right-tending" stroke is a graphic indication of the trait itself: it moves off and away from everything that is in the past, moving toward the future.

Fig. 39: *Initiative as revealed by a strong break-away stroke leaving the baseline.*

AN EXERCISE FOR IMPROVING INITIATIVE

Write: **"start right, act right"** five times per day for thirty days. Concentrate on making strong break-away strokes as illustrated above.

Write out your first day's exercise here. For the next month write your exercises in a notebook acquired for this use alone. After one month, check back here and evaluate your progress.

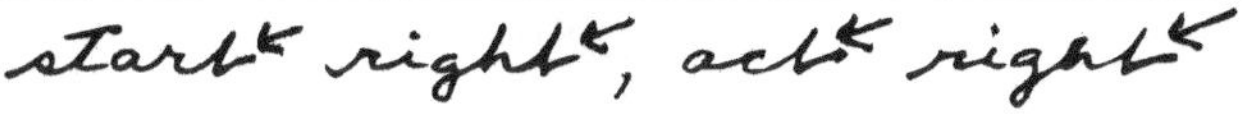

_____

_____

_____

_____

_____

This is an exercise to help you increase your initiative. As you make strong strokes that break away briskly from the baseline in this exercise, consciously remind yourself that you are gaining more initiative with each stroke. *Beyond this exercise, consciously make these break-away strokes whenever you write.*

EXAMPLE

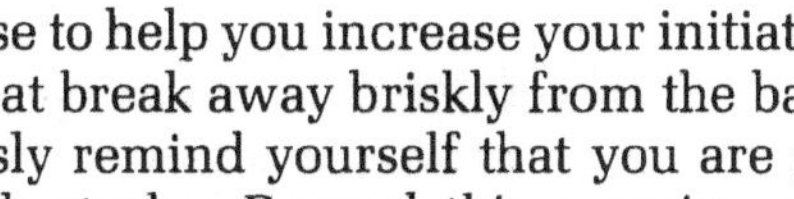

9. ORGANIZATIONAL ABILITY

The heavens, the planets and this centre
Observe degree, priority and place,
Insisture, course, proportion, season, form,
Office and custom, all line of order.

Shakespeare (Troilus and Cressida)

We as human beings, are uniquely able to structure the world in a personally desirable way. **In vocational analysis, one of the first traits a graphoanalyst looks for is organizational ability. In business, it is an essential trait for everyone from the file clerk to the president of the firm.** In any endeavor where teamwork is important, so is organizational ability. Its possessor has the ability to plan strategically, checking each step before taking action.

Fig. 40: *Organizational ability is shown by a balance between the upper and lower loops in "f".*

AN EXERCISE FOR ORGANIZATIONAL ABILITY

Write: **"The gift of organization often fashions fame"** five times per day for thirty days. Balance the upper and lower loops in each "f" that you write.

Write out your first day's exercise here. For the next month write your exercises in a notebook acquired for this use alone. After one month, check back here and evaluate your progress.

_____

_____

_____

_____

_____

The gift of organization often fashions fame.

This is an exercise to help you improve your organizational ability. As you balance your "f's" in this exercise, consciously remind yourself that you are improving your organizational ability with each stroke. *Beyond this exercise, consciously balance your "f" loops whenever you write.*

EXAMPLE   *often effective*

10. IMAGINATION

*The primary imagination I hold to be the living
power and prize spent of all human perception.*

Coleridge

Imagination is necessary for our capacity to look into the future. **If you cannot "imagine" a future, you cannot create a future for yourself. Imagination stirs the emotions, stimulates thinking and spurs action traits.**

Imagination can "give wings to facts." And ideas. Can you build a better mousetrap? Whip up a new kind of cake? Apply centuries-old religious ideas to your contemporary life? Imagination allows you to find new concepts within existing facts and put old ideas to work in new ways.

Philosophical (or **abstract**) *imagination* is shown by the relative size of the loops in the upper zone letters ("b", "d", "f", "h", "k", "l".) The wider the loops, the greater the philosophical imagination.

If you have a large philosophical imagination you are probably drawn to many different philosophies, and this adds meaning to your life. You enjoy thinking about abstract ideas, and your mind tends to gravitate toward the aesthetic realm to put wings on your ideas.

Material imagination is revealed by the lower zone letters ("f", "g", "j", "q" and "y".) The wider the size of the loop in this lower zone, the greater the material imagination. Remember, judge the loop size in relation to other strokes in the handwriting sample.

The lower zone is the "material zone" and reflects our personality as it relates to our bodies, sexual activity, and the physical world around us. A moderate, healthy imagination in this area can be the source of great fulfillment in life. Without imagination, sex would be dull. Imagination stirs the sexual fantasies that can enhance the sexual experience. And with no imagination, social activities such as parties, dates and other get-togethers would be drudgery instead of fun.

Imagination can be taken to the extreme, too. A person with an exaggerated imagination may tend to enlarge experience to the point of distortion. **I want to stress the importance of *balanced* imagination which you can use to transfuse the ordinary things of life with a new perspective.**

To determine the size of imagination in your sample, proceed as follows: measure the width of an "a" or "o" in your handwriting using Gauge #2. *Any upper or lower loop that has a width greater than this indicates above average imagination.*

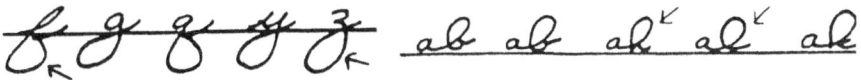

Fig.41: Left, the large lower loops showing MATERIAL IMAGINATION. Right, big upper loops revealing PHILOSOPHICAL IMAGINATION.

AN EXERCISE FOR IMAGINATION

Write: **"flying high in my big imagination"** five times per day for thirty days. Concentrate on making well-shaped loops in each upper and lower zone letter.

Write out your first day's exercise here. For the next month write your exercises in a notebook acquired for this use alone. After one month, check back here and evaluate your progress.

---

flying high in my big imagination

This is an exercise to help you enlarge your imagination. As you work on the upper and lower loops in this exercise, consciously remind yourself that your are magnifying your imagination with each stroke. *Beyond this exercise, consciously adjust your upper and lower loops whenever you write.*

EXAMPLE   *all high*
Day 6

muggy
Day 10

11. DECISIVENESS

Multitudes in the valley of decision.
Joel 3:14

Life confronts us with an endless string of decisions; some are simple, others difficult. The decisive personality has no difficulty in making them all without delay. This decisiveness is graphically portrayed in handwriting by firm final strokes.

If you are decisive, you are resolute in your convictions. People around you recognize you for this gift, and appreciate you too, because you make life easier for the others around you. You eliminate the tension that goes with indecision.

Your ability to make decisions quickly is an economical trait for it avoids wasted time... and often money. It allows you to move adroitly when time is important, sometimes capturing opportunities that others would have missed for lack of a decision. And in making decisions, you communicate your values and convictions clearly to everyone.

Decisiveness makes all other power traits work better. It puts you on a more direct track for achieving your personal goals.

decision

Fig. 42: Notice the firm final strokes of the decisive personality.

AN EXERCISE FOR DECISIVENESS

Write: **"Easy decisions"** five times per day for thirty days. Make sure your final strokes are firm as in the example above.

Write out your first day's exercise here. For the next month write your exercises in a notebook acquired for this use alone. After one month, check back here and evaluate your progress.

_____

_____

_____

_____

_____

Easy decisions

This is an exercise to help you become more decisive. As you make your firm final strokes in this exercise, consciously remind yourself that you are becoming more decisive with each stroke. *Beyond this exercise, consciously firm up your final strokes whenever you write.*

EXAMPLE *Re: Handwriting program*

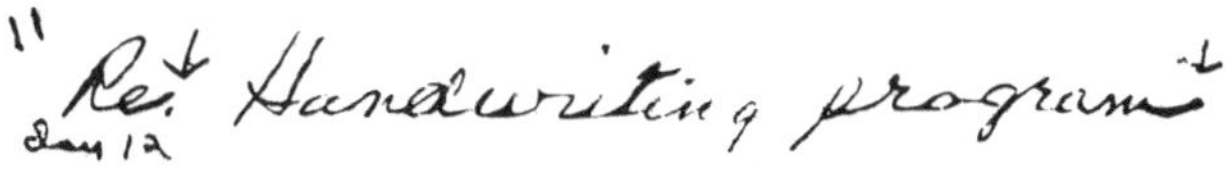

12. DETERMINATION

Here I am and here I stay.

Marshall McMahon
(Battle of Sevastopol)

Determination is the quality of being firm and resolute of purpose. This naturally implies that we *have* some purpose. If your goals are high, you need determination to achieve them.
Determination implies *vigorous action* to achieve your goals. You can "think thin" all you want, but you still have to go on a diet! Determination keeps you on it until you've succeeded — and *strong* determination keeps you from gaining the weight back.

Determination can be revealed in your handwriting. It is seen as a straight stroke below the baseline in the letters "g", "y", "q" and "z".

If the determination stroke is long, the determination will have endurance. A short stroke indicates short endurance.

The weight of the determination stroke must be judged in relation to other strokes in the sample. If it is relatively "heavy," your strength of purpose has power and force behind it! A "light" downstroke reveals weaker determination... although it still may have great endurance.

Fig. 43: Determination is shown by heavy and/or long downstrokes below the baseline.

AN EXERCISE FOR DETERMINATION

Write: **"My z shows my unyielding quality"** five times per day for thirty days. Make the downstrokes below the baseline straight, long and heavy as in the examples above.

Write out your first day's exercise here. For the next month write your exercises in a notebook acquired for this use alone. After one month, check back here and evaluate your progress.

_____

_____

_____

_____

_____

_____

EXAMPLE

This is an exercise to help you increase the power and endurance of your determination. As you make long, heavy downstrokes in this exercise, consciously remind yourself that you are improving your determination with each stroke. Beyond this exercise, consciously make long, heavy downstrokes whenever you write.

13. PERSISTENCE

The heights by great men reached and kept
Were not attained by sudden flight
But they, while their companions slept,
Were toiling upward in the night.

Longfellow
(The Ladder of Saint Augustine)

There is much to be said for "hanging in there." When George Burns was asked what the secret of his success was, he said, "Simple. I outlived everybody."

Persistence is perseverance, not accepting defeat even in the face of tremendous obstacles, "never say die." It is a positive trait that supports success.

Hard work and persistence have succeeded more often than sudden great insights. Perhaps that is why **Thomas Edison said that perspiration was more important than inspiration.**

The "tie" stroke that indicates persistence must have the complete loop to be counted. Please be careful here! The letter "t" is often crossed with a sort of triangular stroke that reaches back to the left making a kind of "star" shape. The "y" and "s" sometimes also show this triangular stroke. It is important not to mistake these common triangular strokes for persistence.

Fig. 44: WRONG. These triangular strokes do NOT show persistence.

Fig. 45: RIGHT. These "tie" loops indicate the persistence trait.

AN EXERCISE FOR PERSISTENCE

Write: **"for every season... turn, turn, turn"** five times per day for thirty days. Strive to make the persistence "tie" in each "f", "s", "t" and "y".

Write out your first day's exercise here. For the next month write your exercises in a notebook acquired for this use alone. After one month, check back here and evaluate your progress.

_____

_____

_____

_____

_____

for every season. . .? turn, turn, turn !

This is an exercise to help you increase your persistence. As you make the persistence "tie" in this exercise, consciously remind yourself that you are gaining persistence with each stroke. *Beyond this exercise, consciously make these persistence "ties" whenever you write.*

EXAMPLE *why do is*

14. DIPLOMACY

*Diplomacy is the art of fishing tranquilly
in troubled water.*

J. Christopher Herold

The diplomat is one who has an understanding of what action or statement is proper or right in any situation. Diplomacy also infers skill in avoiding the word or gesture that would offend or disturb others unnecessarily. The diplomatic person is usually well mannered and perceptive of the attitudes and feelings of other people.

Diplomacy is not something we are born with. It is a wise adaption to the sometimes difficult task of living in harmony with others. Because it is an extension of our care for other people, it should never be misunderstood as manipulation.

Socially, the diplomatic person can be a happy person to be around. When the diplomat is in charge, others seem to do his bidding without resentment or hostility. This occurs not because of manipulation, but because the diplomat puts the needs of the entire group ahead of any selfish motives and deals with people in a non-threatening manner. The real diplomat is always there to remind us of the needs and feelings of people, and so we are encouraged to be nicer to each other.

You may have noticed at every awards ceremony there is always a litany of "thank you's" from the winners. These are truly diplomatic statements that also remind us that world-class success is never achieved alone. The real diplomatic person needs no award or ceremony, however, to prompt a "thank you" to the people who help him.

In the area of selling and persuasion, **diplomacy — a genuine regard for the needs and feelings of others — is indispensable.** A soft diplomatic statement enhances any situation.

Diplomacy is revealed in handwriting by the "m", "n", and the double letter combinations "ll" and "tt". The trait can be identified when the first hump, loop or stem is taller than the next one, giving the letter(s) a slope down to the right.

Fig. 46: Diplomacy is shown by these letters when their tops slope downward to the right.

AN EXERCISE FOR DIPLOMACY

Write: **"all men and women matter"** five times per day for thirty days. Concentrate on the downward slope to the right in each "m", "n", "ll" and "tt".

Write out your first day's exercise here. For the next month write your exercises in a notebook acquired for this use alone. After one month, check back here and evaluate your progress.

_____

_____

_____

_____

This is an exercise to help you improve your diplomacy. As you give a downward slope to each "m", "n", "ll" and "tt" in this exercise, consciously remind yourself that you are gaining diplomacy with each stroke. *Beyond this exercise, consciously give these letters a downward stroke whenever you write.*

EXAMPLE

15. EXPLORATORY THINKING

Of all the thinking processes, this is the most adventuresome. A person who is exploratory in thinking essentially is unafraid to chart new courses and kick over new stones. Such a mind moves out into the unknown with few preconceptions, eager for discovery.

When encountering a problem, this person does not rely merely on the facts as they are known to fashion a solution, but rather sets out to find *missing* information, a *different* approach, and *unknown* relationship between the pieces of the puzzle. Mentally, this person is a discoverer, relishing the new find almost as much as its contribution to a larger whole. Such an intensely curious person never mentally drills a "dry hole" deeper into the ground, preferring instead to drill many holes and cover more ground.

On a social plane, this person can be exciting and invigorating to be with; the **curious mind** has also a curiously stimulating effect on others.

This trait shows up in handwriting as sharp "mountain peaks", almost as if the "explorer" needed them to conquer. These inverted "v" shapes often appear in the letters "h", "m", "n", "p", "w" and sometimes at the top of the "l" loop (which indicates exploratory thinking in the philosophical or abstract area.)

Fig. 47: Exploratory thinking shows as inverted "v's" - or "mountain tops" - in these letters.

AN EXERCISE FOR EXPLORATORY THINKING

Write: **"explore the world of the mind"** five times per day for thirty days. Concentrate on making the sharp "inverted v" shapes as shown in the examples.

Write out your first day's exercise here. For the next month write your exercises in a notebook acquired for this use alone. After one month, check back here and evaluate your progress.

explore the world of the mind.

This is an exercise to help you acquire or sharpen your exploratory thinking. As you make the "inverted v's" in this exercise, consciously remind yourself that you are gaining a more curious and exploratory nature with each stroke. _Beyond this exercise, consciously make these pointed "mountain tops" whenever you write._

EXAMPLE _Dear whoever you are_

16. OPTIMISM

'Twixt the optimist and pessimist
The difference is droll:
The optimist sees the doughnut
But the pessimist sees the hole.

McLandbrugh Wilson
(Optimist and Pessimist)

The healthy optimist believes that generally everything is ordered for the best, or at least leans in the direction of a better tomorrow.

In social situations, the optimist helps to keep the level of discussion on a higher, more positive plane. Since he will believe automatically the best of his fellow man, there will be a refreshing lack of negativity in his conversation. such a person believes anything is possible; bring up a suggestion and you will be faced with a barrage of possibilities. After all, that is what life is all about for the optimist.

The optimist is not immune to life's little surprises, but he is convinced that by his own action he can make things better. This is the bottom line: **the optimist feels he is in control of his life.**

Optimism is an attitude that ensures efficiency. If you spend all your time preparing for the worst, you will not have time to do your best.

Optimism is contagious. Look at two different Presidents, Ronald Reagan and Jimmy Carter. President Carter looked at a nation and saw a malaise sweeping the country coast to coast; Ronald Reagan surveyed the same scene and saw a nation poised for greatness. The election results in 1980 were a triumph for Reagan's eternal optimism. Even voters who disagreed with his ideology decided they liked the positive way in which he expressed it. The optimistic Reagan smile probably swayed as many voters as his speeches.

This is not to say that a cheery attitude can substitute for wisdom, clear thinking, and high values and goals. But success or failure sometimes can hinge on that one important trait: optimism.

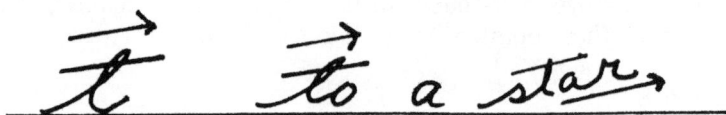

Fig. 48: *Optimism is shown by upslanted "t" crossings and upturned final strokes.*

AN EXERCISE FOR OPTIMISM

Write: **"Hitch your wagon to a star!" (Emerson said this first, but I always like to add: "... and others will follow.")** Write it five times per day for thirty days. Make your "t" crossings and final strokes slant upwards as in the examples above.

Write out your first day's exercise here. For the next month write your exercises in a notebook acquired for this use alone. After one month, check back here and evaluate your progress.

_____

_____

_____

_____

This is an exercise to help you increase your optimism. As you cross your "t's" and make upslanted words in this exercise, consciously remind yourself that you are becoming more optimistic with each stroke. *Beyond this exercise, consciously adjust your "t" crossings and final strokes whenever you write.*

17. TALKATIVENESS

The four-letter word for psychotherapy is TALK.

Eric Hodgins
(Episode)

Talkativeness is a trait that we are often ambivalent about. It seems that nobody talks just enough; everyone is judged for talking too much or too little. The healthy talker loves conversation rather than monologues; what good is talk without feedback, anyway?

A glance at your handwriting may give you a better clue as to your mental desire to share with others via talking. If certain letters that are normally closed are left open in your handwriting ("a", "d", "g", "o" and "q"), you undoubtedly like to talk more than the average person.

In therapy, talk is often very good. Some time ago at Stanford University, an interesting experiment took place. The student mental health clinic was overloaded and there was a long waiting list. It was decided that a certain number of students would be divided into three groups: one group received professional psychotherapy; a control group received no therapy; and a third group met regularly to talk with English majors.

Can you see it coming? After six months the three groups were tested and compared to see what progress they had made toward solving their problems. Those who received professional psychotherapy were a little better off statistically than those who received no therapy at all. The clear winners in the experiment, however, were those who were allowed and encouraged to *talk* even though no professional psychotherapy was involved.

The importance of this should not be underestimated. **Too often emotional problems arise in our lives because communication with others has been cut off.** We begin to feel that we are alone in the world, that no one else has problems like we have.

According to polls, the most common fear among us is the fear of speaking in front of a group. We all have a bit of reticence with people we do not know well, and increasing the number of people to whom we must speak only increases our anxiety. More often than not, however, groups are eager for a speaker to do well and forgiving of imperfections. The fear, then, is irrational but very real nevertheless. There is one effective way to overcome it, though; speak in public as often as possible and the fear gradually fades. **Graphotherapy can be a first step in the direction of your opening up.**

Being able to speak, not only in groups but one-to-one as well, is indispensable for any king of success.

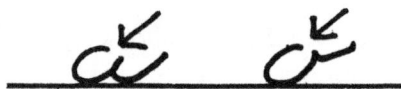

Fig. 49: Talkativeness is shown by open letters that are normally closed.

A person with an abundance of open letters, as in the example above, has a mental desire to communicate by talking. Most often such a person behaves by talking often and in great quantity, but sometimes a person with this trait will "edit himself", becoming more reticent. The desire is still there, but the individual — for some reason — chooses consciously or subconsciously not to speak in a "talkative" way.

The opposite is sometimes true, too. If your "a's", "o's", etc., are closed, this usually means you are reticent to speak. You may talk a lot, however, which may indicate that your talkativeness is a "cover-up" for something else. **Handwriting shows the inner you (subconscious)**, which is not always honestly expressed through behavior. As in-depth handwriting analysis can often reveal the reasons for a discrepancy between the traits you have and the behavior you show.

AN EXERCISE FOR TALKATIVENESS

Write: **"a good talk is good thought on the run"** five times per day for thirty days. Make a conscious effort to leave the loops open on each "a", "d", "g" and "o".

Write out your first day's exercise here. For the next month write your exercises in a notebook acquired for this use alone. After one month, check back here and evaluate your progress.

_____

_____

_____

_____

_____

a good talk is a good thought on the run.

EXAMPLE

This is an exercise to help you improve your desire to communicate with others verbally. As you leave "open" certain letters in this exercise, consciously remind yourself that you are becoming more talkative with each stroke. *Beyond this exercise, consciously leave "open" letters whenever you write.*

EXAMPLE 

18. SENSE OF HUMOR

Humor is emotional chaos remembered in tranquility.
James Thurber

James Thurber said that a sense of humor allows us to look back on even the hardest experiences in life and find some perspective, perhaps something to chuckle about.

We all have met people who have no sense of humor. A joke or light-hearted comment is met with an icy stare, and anything that is not totally serious is ignored. There seems to be something "dead" in these personalities. There seems to be some sort of life force missing.

On the other hand, there is the personality with such an exaggerated sense of humor that everything is the subject of laughter and jokes. Nothing is taken seriously. Laughter and fun are used to fend off deep consideration of important matters.

A good sense of humor is as valuable asset, but balance is the key. You must be your own judge here in determining what you have to work on.

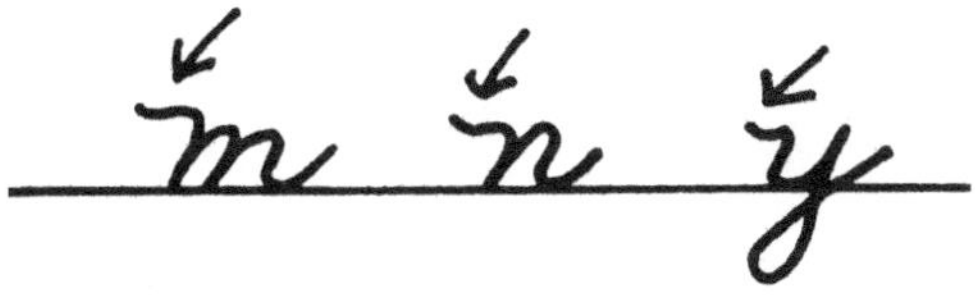

Fig. 50: Humor is shown by a flourish in an initial handwriting stroke.

AN EXERCISE FOR HUMOR

Write: ***"Humor is our greatest national resource"*** five times per day for thirty days. Concentrate on making initial strokes that contain the "humor" flourish.

Write out your first day's exercise here. For the next month write your exercises in a notebook acquired for this use alone. After one month, check back here and evaluate your progress.

_____

_____

_____

_____

_____

humor is our greatest national resource.

This is an exercise to help you change your attitude toward your goals in life. As you make the "humor flourish" in this exercise, consciously remind yourself that you are improving your sense with each stroke. *Beyond this exercise, consciously add this "humor flourish" whenever you write.*

EXAMPLE *my mother is humorous*

19. BROADMINDED

I love to lose myself in other's minds.

Charles Lamb

The healthy open mind is like a fertile field ready to be sown. Ideas like seeds can easily take root there and grow. A closed mind is a rocky wasteland; ideas have nowhere to take hold and sprout.

Broadmindedness shows in your handwriting. Look for fat, circular loops in such lower zone letters as "a", "e" and "o". (Skinny, strangulated formations show the opposite trait, narrowmindedness.)

The broadminded couple will be able to express themselves to each other without censoring themselves and with no embarrassment. **Open minds usually accompany open lines of communication.**

If you are a broadminded person, you will find yourself at ease in a wide variety of social situations. Allowing yourself to remain "open" to others and their ideas gives you more opportunities for fulfilling friendships and lasting relationships in life. Without a value system with which to make final judgments, however, broadmindedness can lead to indecision, confusion or an "anything goes" lifestyle that lacks direction.

In business, broadmindedness is an asset as well; it is often wiser to listen with an open mind to others before making decisions. A broadminded person is not threatened by new ideas, perspectives or horizons. The healthy open mind sifts through such new notions, thinking of them as exciting options that can suggest new solutions.

Fig 51: *Broadmindedness is revealed by fat, round formations in the letters "a", "e", "o".*

AN EXERCISE FOR BROADMINDEDNESS

Write: **"a broad, open mind learns often"** five times per day for thirty days. Concentrate on making each "a", "e" and "o" fat and round.

Write out your first day's exercise here. For the next month write your exercises in a notebook acquired for this use alone. After one month, check back here and evaluate your progress.

This is an exercise to help you become more broadminded. As you make fat, round middle zone strokes in this exercise, consciously remind yourself that you are becoming more open minded with each stroke. *Beyond this exercise, consciously make these middle zone letters well rounded whenever you write.*

EXAMPLE

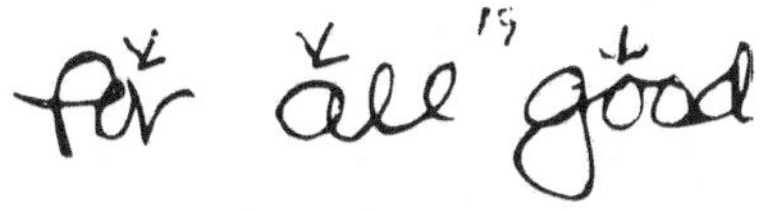

20. LOYALTY

No, the heart that has truly lov'd never forgets,
But as truly loves on to the close...

Thomas Moore
(Believe Me, If All Those Endearing Young Charms)

Loyalty can be the noblest of all traits. The loyal person is always steadfast in what he thinks is right, what he truly believes. We admire that in people because we sense that loyalty to oneself implies loyalty to others. In handwriting, loyalty is evidenced by round, firm "i" dots.

Loyalty is a quality we require in all those closest to us. People who are constant and faithful in their relations with us inspire the same loyalty they have shown.

Intense, exaggerated loyalty, though can be a dangerous thing. **Loyalty without values is worthless.** As mentioned earlier, the handwriting of **Sirhan Sirhan** plainly betrayed how loyal he was. Unfortunately, **his loyalty** was **misplaced and the consequences were tragic.**

Fig. 52: Round, firm "i" dots show loyalty.

AN EXERCISE FOR LOYALTY

Write: **"Faith in friends is important"** five times per day for thirty days. Consciously make each "i" dot round and firm.

Write out your first day's exercise here. For the next month write your exercises in a notebook acquired for this use alone. After one month, check back here and evaluate your progress.

EXAMPLE

This is an exercise to help you become more loyal. As you make firm, round "i" dots in this exercise, consciously remind yourself that you are gaining loyalty with each stroke. *Beyond this exercise, consciously make the i dot letters well rounded whenever you write.*

lift in depth

21. MANUAL DEXTERITY

Help, Hands, for I have no Lands.

Benjamin Franklin
(Poor Richard's Almanac)

When we speak of **dexterity**, I am referring to the general idea of **"handness,"** because that is what dexterity has come to mean. In the strictest sense, **manual dexterity means cleverness with the hands**. In a sexual context, though, it means skill or ease in using the hands or the body. Since we do not wish to turn this book into "The Joy of Sex," I will leave you to draw your own conclusions.

When Ben Franklin said, "Help, Hands, for I have no Lands", he spoke from experience. He was not wealthy as a young man. It was by the skill of his own hands that he made his fortune and turned himself into the person he became.

As a printer's apprentice, Franklin was faster than all the older, more experienced typesetters. As a tinkerer, he would come up with little inventions that would make him more productive, and later would make him his fortune.

With clever hands, riches and lands will come.

m̃ ñ r̃

Fig 53: *Manual dexterity is revealed by rounded "m's and "n's", and flat-topped "r's".*

AN EXERCISE FOR MANUAL DEXTERITY

Write: **'My times are in thy hand" (Psalms 31:15)** five times per day for thirty days. Concentrate on making each "m" and "n" rounded on the top, and each "r" flat-topped.

Write out your first day's exercise here. For the next month write your exercises in a notebook acquired for this use alone. After one month, check back here and evaluate your progress.

My Times are in thy hands.

This is an exercise to help you increase your manual dexterity. As you make the fat, round middle zone strokes in this exercise, consciously remind yourself that you are gaining dexterity with each stroke. *Beyond this exercise, consciously round your "m's" and "n's" and make flat-topped "r's" whenever you write.*

strangers   Monticell,

EXAMPLE

22. GENEROSITY

Behold, I do not give lectures or a little charity.
When I give, I give myself.

Walt Whitman
(Leaves of Grass)

True generosity is shown not only by giving and sharing what we have, but by a nature that is free of pettiness. **Generosity is characterized by warmth, sympathy, and tenderness. The truly generous person is a cheerful giver.** There is no concern that the gift has diminished the giver in any way; there is no feeling of duty in the giving.

Often we fall in love first because we have perceived that the object of our affections is generous. Usually it is the kind of generosity that expresses itself in giving of gifts, material things, even time. A generosity of spirit is what holds us to the ones we love. A giving lover is a wise lover. The giving lover has learned the oldest human lessons. You can call it karma or you can just say "what goes around, comes around." What you give (good or bad) you will also receive in return.

> *And in the end..*
> *The love you get*
> *Is equal to the love*
> *You make.*
>
> *The Beatles*

The generous friend liberally shares time and advice. He is always there when help is needed. The generous friend is wise. He, too, knows the way of the world:

A man there was, And they called him mad: The more he gave, The more he had.

Fig. 54: *Generosity is shown by final strokes that are at least as long as the preceding letter before turning upward.*

AN EXERCISE FOR GENEROSITY

Write: **"When I give, I give myself"** five times per day for thirty days. Concentrate on making the final strokes at least as long as the preceding letter is wide before turning the stroke upward.

Write out your first day's exercise here. For the next month write your exercises in a notebook acquired for this use alone. After one month, check back here and evaluate your progress.

_____

_____

_____

_____

_____

This is an exercise to help you increase your generosity. As you make the long upward final strokes in this exercise, consciously remind yourself that you are becoming more generous with each stroke. Beyond this exercise, *consciously make these long upward final strokes whenever you write.*

EXAMPLE -

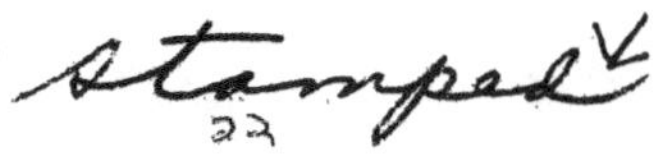

Elayne V. Lindberg with Gary Lindberg

23. GOOD SELF-CONTROL

Reader, attend! whether thy soul
Soars fancy's flights beyond the pole,
Or darkly grubs this earthly hole in low pursuit;
Know *prudent cautious self-control*
Is wisdom's root.

Burns
(A Bard's Epitaph)

Very little is accomplished without some self-control. The person who is overly emotional, prone to flying off the handle, who cannot master himself in any way, probably will find this book useless. A certain amount of self-control is necessary.

Self-control, in a sexual sense, means the habit of having ones energies and emotions under control of the will. This is not to say that all emotion is negative, of course, but that **control of emotion is the beginning of wisdom.**

And, speaking of husbands...

I always thought that my husband was much less emotional than I was. He was usually cool and calm, while I was always getting upset. When I began studying handwriting, I discovered that he was much more emotional than I was, but he had learned to *control* his emotions. When I learned how emotional he was, I respected him even more for his control.

Fig. 55: Self-control is shown by "t" crossings that look like an upside-down wash basin.

AN EXERCISE FOR SELF-CONTROL

Write: **"total control"** five times per day for thirty days. Concentrate on making each "t" crossing upside down wash basin.

Write out your first day's exercise here. For the next month write your exercises in a notebook acquired for this use alone. After one month, check back here and evaluate your progress.

_____

_____

_____

_____

_____

total control

This is an exercise to help you gain more self-control. As you make upside down basin-shaped "t" crossings in this exercise, consciously remind yourself that you are gaining self-control with each stroke. *Beyond this exercise, consciously make these upside down wash basin-shaped "t" crossings whenever you write.*

EXAMPLE *at the top*

24. LOVES PHYSICAL ACTIVITY

Love's mysteries in souls do grow,
And yet the body is his book.

John Donne

(The Extasie)

Today more than ever, physical fitness is being pursued by Americans of all ages. Studies have shown that those who exercise regularly live longer and healthier lives. Everything seems better when you have your health.

A desire for physical activity can result in the classic ideal of the "sound mind in a sound body." The bodily ease and grace that comes from exercise and physical activity also goes a long way toward making us more attractive to the opposite sex, but there is an added benefit: we become more at ease with ourselves.

When we feel strong, fit, and attractive, we send out positive messages to all around us. Others begin to respond to us more positively as a result. This positive aura, ease, and grace is commonly known as "sex appeal." It is the essence of physical attraction.

Needless to say, a healthy body leads to a healthy outlook that is a positive base for everything we do in life.

The desire for physical activity may not always be manifest in behavior, however. Again, the handwriting stroke (large lower loop in the "p") reveals the inner trait, not the outward behavior. An individual may be too busy for activity, *have physical handicaps* or an illness, or even be repressing the expression of this desire for some reason. In some cases, the individual with this trait may satisfy the desire in a Walter Mitty-like fashion through *watching* sports activities.

Fig. 56: A love of physical activity is shown by large lower loops in the letter "p". The width of the loop must be wider than the closest "e" or "a".

AN EXERCISE FOR PHYSICAL ACTIVITY

Write: **"physical people perchance persist"** five times per day for thirty days. Concentrate on making large lower loops in each letter "p".

Write out your first day's exercise here. For the next month write your exercises in a notebook acquired for this use alone. After one month, check back here and evaluate your progress.

_____

_____

_____

_____

This is an exercise to help you develop a greater desire for physical activity. As you make large lower "p" loops in this exercise, consciously remind yourself that you are gaining more of a love for physical activity with each stroke. Beyond this exercise, consciously make large lower loops in your "p's" whenever you write.

24 EXAMPLE

25. INTUITIVE THINKING

...One in whom persuasion and belief
Had ripened into faith, and faith become
A passionate intuition.

William Wordsworth

Intuitiveness gives its possessor insight into problems or relationships. It is an uncanny knowing of things not revealed by facts or other evidence. Intuition, once developed is a great aid to all other thinking processes. In handwriting, it is shown by a break between connecting letters in a word. It is almost as if the mind of the intuitive writer hesitates or perceives solutions without knowing how this knowledge is acquired.

Intuition gives people a "sixth sense" about the truthfulness of things, the genuine quality of a person, even the likelihood of success of a particular endeavor. It is a clue, a revelation, an inkling that nudges the mind in one direction or the other. It brings to the surface a nearly psychic insight that makes use of all one's senses plus something quite undefinable, as if the mind has become a divining rod drawing all other faculties toward ultimate truth or solution.

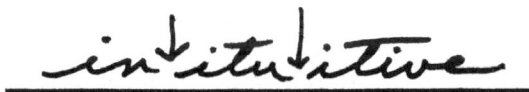

Fig. 57: Intuitive thinking is shown by frequent breaks between letter structures.

AN EXERCISE FOR INTUITIVE THINKING

Write: **"my intuition is being developed"** five times per day for thirty days. Concentrate on making breaks between many of the letters in these words without resorting to printing.

Write out your first day's exercise here. For the next month write your exercises in a notebook acquired for this use alone. After one month, check back here and evaluate your progress.

_____

_____

_____

_____

This is an exercise to help you improve your intuitiveness. As you make breaks between letters in this exercise, consciously remind yourself that you are becoming more intuitive with each stroke. Beyond this exercise, consciously make breaks between letter structures whenever you write.   EXAMPLE

26. LOGICAL THINKING

"Contrariwise," continued Tweedledee,
"If it was so, it might be;
and if it were so, it would be.
But it isn't, so it ain't.
That's logic."

Lewis Carroll

A logical thinker considers ideas in his mind before he expresses them. Such a person thinks thoroughly and accurately. He follows directions carefully and has the ability to do so. Good, sound judgments come from logical thinking, sometimes called "cumulative" thinking because it requires the accumulation of information to provide the basis for orderly judgment. **People who think in a logical way fall in love with their minds first; the heart follows after much consideration.** The brain may think lightening-fast but decisions are made carefully. In handwriting, logical thinking is shown by the same strokes that reveal manual dexterity (flat-top "r's" and rounded tops on "m's" and "n's".)

Fig. 58: Logical thinking is revealed by flat-topped "r's" and rounded "m's" and "n's".

AN EXERCISE FOR LOGICAL THINKING

Write: **"my thinking is orderly"** five times per day for thirty days. Concentrate on making each "r" with a flat top and each "m" and "n" rounded on each hump.

Write out your first day's exercise here. For the next month write your exercises in a notebook acquired for this use alone. After one month, check back here and evaluate your progress.

_____

_____

_____

_____

my thinking is orderly.

This is an exercise to help you improve or acquire logical thinking. As you make round "m's" and "n's", and flat-topped "r's" in this exercise, consciously remind yourself that your thinking is becoming more logical and orderly with each stroke. *Beyond this exercise, consciously adjust these middle zone letters whenever you write.*

EXAMPLE *come to wider*

27. GOOD COLOR SENSE

If you exhibit this trait in your handwriting, **love of color —** **vibrant colors —** excites you. Pastel colors calm you. All colors are meaningful. You have an innate sense about what colors look good together. Color makes you feel alive.

This trait also indicates that all of your senses are acute. You love good food, music, art, sex — anything involving your senses: seeing, hearing, smelling, touching, tasting.

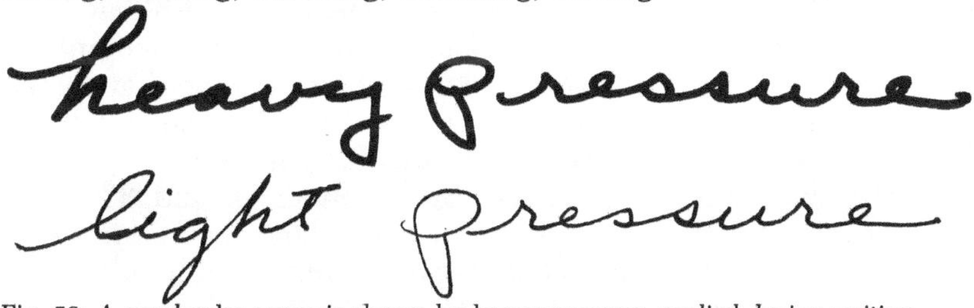

heavy pressure

light pressure

Fig. 59: A good color sense is shown by heavy pressure applied during writing.

AN EXERCISE FOR GOOD COLOR SENSES

Write: **"I love vivid colors"** five times per day for thirty days. Concentrate on writing with heavier than normal pressure so all the words are bold and the strokes heavy.

Write out your first day's exercise here. For the next month write your exercises in a notebook acquired for this use alone. After one month, check back here and evaluate your progress.

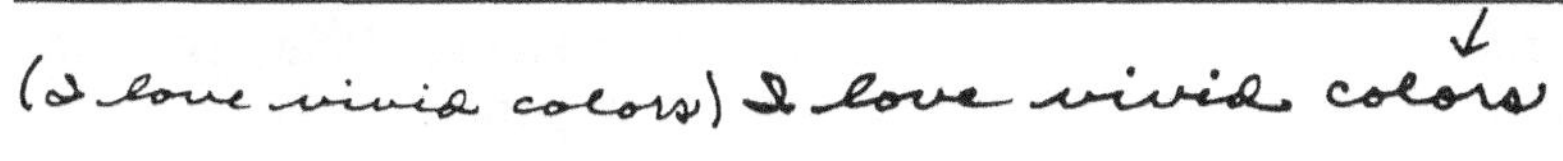

_____

_____

_____

_____

_____

(I love vivid colors) I love vivid colors

This is an exercise to help you develop your color sense. As you write heavier than normal in this exercise, consciously remind yourself that you are developing more of a color sense with each stroke. *Beyond this exercise, consciously use heavier pressure whenever you write.*

EXAMPLE *Kmom ;*

attn: Elain Lindberg

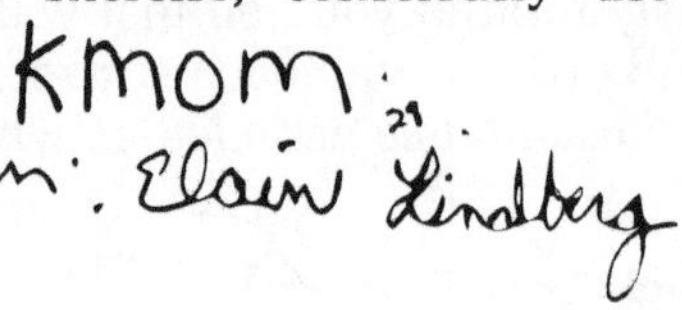

28. INDEPENDENT THINKING

The universe is transformation
Our life is what our thoughts make it.

Marcus Aurelius

Independent thinking is the first step to original, creative thinking. If this trait occurs in your handwriting, it indicates you have the ability to draw your own conclusions and come up with original ideas. You are seldom influenced by past customs or tradition, choosing instead to think things through in a fresh way. The opinions of others affect your decisions only when these opinions make sense to you. While you may accept information that comes to you, conclusions made by other people influence you very little. **You are a person who genuinely thinks for yourself.**

Independent thinking is revealed by the letters "d" and "t". If the upper portion of a "d" stem — that portion above the middle zone loop — is short in relation to the height of companion middle zone letters, it indicates independent thinking. The trait is also indicated by "t" stems that are the same height (or only slightly taller) than companion middle zone letters.

start today

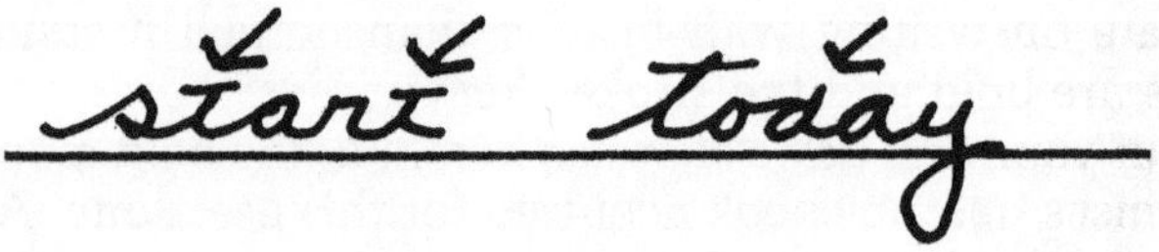

Fig. 60: Independent thinking is shown by extremely short "d" and "t" stems.

AN EXERCISE FOR INDEPENDENT THINKING

Write: **"short stems denote independent thought"** five times per day for thirty days. Concentrate on making each "t" and "d" stem short as described above.

Write out your first day's exercise here. For the next month write your exercises in a notebook acquired for this use alone. After one month, check back here and evaluate your progress.

_____

_____

_____

_____

_____

short stems denote independent thought

This is an exercise to help you think more independently. As you make short "d" and "t" stems in this exercise, consciously remind yourself that you are gaining the ability to think more independently with each stroke. *Beyond this exercise, consciously make these "d" and "t" stems very short whenever you write.*

EXAMPLE *short details*

29. LITERARY INCLINATION

To find this trait in a handwriting sample is to discover one of the most positive indications. A letter "e" that is written like a "capital E" in the middle of a word reveals literary inclination in the writer. This "Greek E" shows an individual who loves literature and many of the finer things of life, and who desires to improve in the loftier planes of thinking and living.

The so-called "delta d" also reveals this trait, as does any lower zone loop that resembles a "figure 8." If the maker of these strokes is not a "writer" as such, then at least he appreciates good writing. **Note** the potential for writing could be developed.

Delta   Greek E   Literary

Fig. 61: Literary inclination is shown by "delta d's', "Greek E's', and a lower loop formation that looks like an "8'.

AN EXERCISE FOR LITERARY INCLINATION

Write: **"delta d and Greek E give literary desire"** five times per day for thirty days. Concentrate on making "delta d's", "Greek E's" and lower loops "8's".

Write out your first day's exercise here. For the next month write your exercises in a notebook acquired for this use alone. After one month, check back here and evaluate your progress.

_____

_____

_____

_____

_____

Delta d and Greek e give literary desire

This is an exercise to help you develop literary inclination. As you make the proper strokes in this exercise, consciously remind yourself that you are becoming more attuned to writing and literature with each stroke. *Beyond this exercise, consciously make these strokes whenever you write.*

EXAMPLE

30. PURSUE ARTISTIC AREA

It is the glory and the good of art,
That Art remains the one way possible
Of speaking truth,
To minds like mine at least.

Robert Browning

There are many ways of pursuing artistic areas. It may involve the creation of art itself. It may take the form of a deep and fulfilling appreciation of art. For the artist, art is expression: a message sent. To the observer or collector, it is a message received. The "experience" of art is perhaps one of the most profound of all, and so it is not surprising that some people live their lives for art. And yet not all of us share this experience or the desire for it.

Evidence of artistic pursuits can be found in handwriting samples. Look for the same strokes that identify literary inclinations: the "delta d, Greek E," and the "figure 8" formation in lower loops.

Fig. 62: Artistic pursuits are shown by "delta d's", "Greek e's", and a lower loop formation that looks like an "8".

AN EXERCISE FOR ARTISTIC PURSUIT

Write: **"delta d and Greek e give artistic desire"** five times per day for thirty days. Concentrate on making "delta d's", "Greek e's" and lower loop "8's'.

Write out your first day's exercise here. For the next month write your exercises in a notebook acquired for this use alone. After one month, check back here and evaluate your progress.

_____

_____

_____

_____

_____

Delta d and Greek E give literary desire.

This is an exercise to help you achieve stronger artistic pursuits. As you make the directed strokes in this exercise, consciously remind yourself that you are gaining strength in this area with each stroke. Beyond this exercise, consciously make these strokes whenever you write.

master of none and therefore new toward any one.

EXAMPLE

Literary ability

THE
RED FLAGS
AND
GRAPHOTHERAPY
EXERCISES

1. OVERLY SENSITIVE

...the pain
Of fancied scorn and undeserved disdain...
Of needless shame, and self-imposed disgrace...

William Cowper
(Conversation)

If you are an *overly sensitive* person — and **I emphasize overly sensitive — your feelings are easily affected by other people and outside events. You have antennae that reach out all the time to catch even the subtlest communication that may concern you.**

Sensitivity in the right proportion can be a positive trait, leading us to dignity, love, appreciation of art and the finer things in life. But too much of it combined with an active imagination can lead to trouble. Imagined slights suddenly become bitter arguments (or repressed hurt) because an overly sensitive person tends to imagine the worst.

In social situations it is usually the fear of ridicule that makes us clam up in hyper-sensitive silence. Repeated hurts, real or imagined, train us over time to be alert to any hint of criticism. If our imaginations are not overly inflated and running at full throttle, however, it's not hard to see that there's more good will out there than we thought. In fact, an objective view of most situations will reveal that most people are not staring at us or criticizing us; alas, they are probably *ignoring* us!

An overly sensitive person is at a disadvantage in accomplishing productive and creative work. Too much time and mental energy is wasted on imagining the criticisms to come. This uses valuable time and creates a timid, passive individual too afraid of censure to create.

A fat, wide "d" loop shows a person who is sensitive about his or her *appearance.* If this "d" stem loop is wider than the closest "e" or "a", the writer is *overly* sensitive about appearance. The fatter the loop, the more sensitive the writer.

Sometimes a writer will make a loop out of the "t" stem. A fat, wide "t" stem loop shows a person who is sensitive about his or her *career, job, or tasks being done.* If this "t" loop is wider than the closest "e" or "a", the writer is *overly* sensitive. Again, the wider the loop, the more sensitive the writer.

Fig. 63: Wide, fat loops in the stems of "d's" and "t's" indicate over-sensitivity.

STEP ONE: *AN EXERCISE TO DECREASE OVER-SENSITIVITY*

Write: **"today I demand untwisted truth"** five times per day for thirty days. Concentrate on making each "d" and "t" stem loop slimmer. The "d" loop should be no fatter than the width of a companion "e" or "a", and the "t" loop should be no more than half that width.

Write out your first day's exercise here. For the next month write your exercises in a notebook acquired for this use alone. After one month, check back here and evaluate your progress.

_____

_____

_____

_____

_____

This is an exercise to help you decrease your over-sensitivity. As you make slimmer "d" and "t" loops in this exercise, consciously remind yourself that you are becoming less sensitive with each stroke. *Beyond this exercise, consciously make these adjustments whenever you write.*

STEP TWO: *ACQUIRE SELF-RELIANCE*

After a month of the above practice, you should begin an exercise to develop a POWER TRAIT that helps to counterbalance this RED FLAG. If your handwriting does not show **SELF-RELIANCE,** look up the exercise for developing this trait. Eliminating a RED FLAG is best accomplished in a two-step program: 1) eradicating the negative stroke; and 2) developing a POWER TRAIT to fill a deficit that allowed the negative trait to form.

2. RESENTMENT

To ruminate upon evils, to make critical notes upon injuries, and be too acute in their apprehension, is to add unto our own tortures, to feather the arrows of our enemies, and to resolve to sleep no more.

Sir *Thomas Browne*

In handwriting analysis, one of the most negative strokes is the one revealing RESENTMENT. This RED FLAG is so damaging because it robs us of time and energy. **Unchecked, it can steal from us the joy of living.**

In a relationship, a constant feeling of "being imposed upon" can lead to resentment, strangling our sense of fun and spontaneity. Resentful relationships cannot last; either the resentment goes, or the relationship does. Most often we walk away from people and situations that cause us to feel resentment.

Whether the injury or injustice that causes our resentment is real or imagined, the resentment itself is usually the culprit that makes us the loser; we lose a friend and the possibility for personal growth by rising above the circumstance. We lose the fulfillment that can come from forgiveness. And although our dignity seemed to have been threatened by this outside force, we lose the *genuine* dignity that comes from having conquered resentment (and the indignity it causes by negatively influencing our behavior.)

With a little thought, you can identify what people or things in your life you resent. Abandoning resentment is a way of taking control of your life and coming to peace with yourself.

Resentment is betrayed in handwriting by the inflexible initial stroke on many letters. If you see it, you can start to eliminate it through the exercise below. Because resentment can show in so many letters, however, to conquer this RED FLAG requires an *especially diligent* effort to eliminate the stroke from all your daily writing, not just in the exercise. Until the stroke is gone from your handwriting, continually search each new writing you make for resentment and remind yourself to consciously eliminate the rigid, straight initial stroke that is so negative.

Fig. 64: Resentment is shown by an inflexible, straight initial stroke that rises from the baseline (or below.)

STEP ONE: AN EXERCISE TO DECREASE RESENTMENT

Write: **"I need to bend my initial strokes"** five times per day for thirty days. Concentrate on making each initial stroke curved, not straight. On the "m" and "n", give the initial stroke a little flourish as in the example **below.**

Write out your first day's exercise here. For the next month write your exercises in a notebook acquired for this use alone. After one month, check back here and evaluate your progress.

_____

_____

_____

_____

_____

This is an exercise to help you decrease your resentment. As you bend each initial stroke in this exercise, consciously remind yourself that you are becoming less resentful with each stroke. Beyond this exercise, consciously make these adjustments whenever you write.

STEP TWO: ACQUIRE GREATER OPTIMISM

After a month of the above practice, you should begin an exercise to develop a POWER TRAIT that helps to counterbalance this RED FLAG. If your handwriting does not show **OPTIMISM,** look up the exercise for developing this trait. Greater optimism helps you see the positive side of persons or situations you have come to resent, making it easier to conquer resentment. Eliminating a RED FLAG is best accomplished in a two-step program: 1) eradicating the negative stroke; and 2) developing a POWER TRAIT to fill a deficit that allowed the negative trait to form.

3. SELF-CONSCIOUS

Trust thyself: *every heart vibrates to that iron strong.*

Ralph Waldo Emerson
(Self-Reliance)

Being self-conscious can affect all areas of your performance. This trait is evidence that your concept of yourself is based upon approval or disapproval of others.

To eliminate self-consciousness from your life, go back and study all the many positive traits you have identified in your handwriting. Put away your negative thoughts. Go forward!

Self-consciousness is *fear*. Fear of the opinions of others. Fear of not being good enough. Fear of appearing or being strange, different, unique. You do not need this fear in your life. YOUR UNIQUENESS IS POSITIVE! You should not look like someone else, but like yourself! You should compliment yourself on your positive traits, skills and talents.

Self-consciousness shows in your handwriting as uneven humps in the "m" or "n", the left hump being lower. Likewise, if the tops of two "l's" or two "t's" written together slant down to the left (or a "tl" or "lt", for that matter) you have also identified self-consciousness.

Fig. 65: Self-consciousness is shown by lower humps in the "m" and "n", and "ll's", "tt's", "lt's" and "tl's" that slant to the left.

STEP ONE: AN EXERCISE TO
DECREASE SELF-CONSCIOUSNESS

Write: **"make even humps in all letters"** five times per day for thirty days. Concentrate on making the humps in each "m" and "n" even in height — or lower on the right (which develops the trait of DIPLOMACY. The "ll's" and "tt's" should also have level tops or slope to the right (DIPLOMACY here, too.)

Write out your first day's exercise here. For the next month write your exercises in a notebook acquired for this use alone. After one month, check back here and evaluate your progress.

---

make even humps in all letters

This is an exercise to help you decrease your self-consciousness. As you make the writing adjustments in this exercise, consciously remind yourself that you are becoming less self-conscious with each stroke. *Beyond this exercise, consciously make these adjustments whenever you write.*

STEP TWO: ACQUIRE GOOD CONFIDENCE

After a month of the above practice, you should begin an exercise to develop a POWER TRAIT that helps to counterbalance this RED FLAG. If your handwriting does not show **GOOD CONFIDENCE,** look up the exercise for developing this trait. Eliminating a RED FLAG is best accomplished in a two-step program: 1) eradicating the negative stroke; and 2) developing a POWER TRAIT to fill a deficit that allowed the negative trait to form.

4. PROCRASTINATION

Procrastination is the art of keeping up with yesterday.

Donald Marquis

Procrastination is a common reaction to pressure. The most common reason for "putting things off" is the fear of failure. What is not completed cannot be judged. If you don't act, you can't fail.

The other side of this coin is all too apparent: if you don't act, you can't succeed.

While we procrastinate, life speeds by. Procrastinating does not make you an automatic failure, **but it certainly puts success in a holding pattern.**

In handwriting, procrastination is revealed by "t" crossings that start to the left of the stem and never get there.

The stem remains uncrossed, just as jobs remain undone. Look also for "i's" that are dotted to the left of the stem, never quite getting to where they belong.

Fig. 66: Procrastination is revealed by "t" crossings and "i" dots to the left of the stem.

STEP ONE: *AN EXERCISE TO DECREASE PROCRASTINATION*

Write: **"initiative eliminates procrastination"** five times per day for thirty days. Concentrate on crossing each "t" and dotting each "i" directly above the stem.

Write out your first day's exercise here. For the next month write your exercises in a notebook acquired for this use alone. After one month, check back here and evaluate your progress.

_____

_____

_____

_____

_____

This is an exercise to help you decrease your procrastination. As you cross your "t" stems and dot the "i's" above the stems in this exercise, consciously remind yourself that you are becoming less inclined to procrastinate with each stroke. *Beyond this exercise, consciously make these adjustments whenever you write.*

STEP TWO: *ACQUIRE GREATER INITIATIVE*

After a month of the above practice, you should begin an exercise to develop a POWER TRAIT that helps to counterbalance this RED FLAG, If your handwriting does not show **INITIATIVE,** look up the exercise for developing this trait. Eliminating a RED FLAG is best accomplished in a two-step program: 1) eradicating the negative stroke; and 2) developing a POWER TRAIT to fill a deficit that allowed the negative trait to form.

5. TEMPER

Anyone can become angry — that is easy;
but to be angry with the right person,
to the right degree, at the right time,
for the right purpose, and in the right way —
that is not easy.

Aristotle

Anger is an emotion. Temper is a personality trait or "tick." When one possesses this trait, temper is the first to flare but anger follows closely on its heels. **The potential for temper is innate in all of us. Look at a baby; shortly after birth we can see anger in a cry for hunger or a wet diaper.**

Watch closely for the temper tick in your handwriting. While we all have a temper, finding this stroke indicates that your boiling point is lower and your temper hotter than average. If you find it, it's up to you to determine where your anger is coming from and how to control it. Ask yourself: why am I on the verge of anger so often? Then work to modify this stroke in your writing. The temper tick is revealed in handwriting by a short, straight initial stroke on a letter.

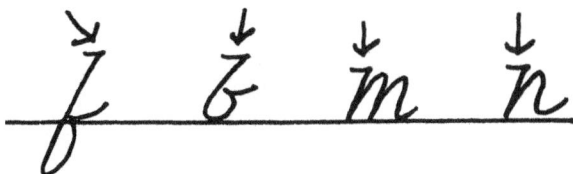

Fig. 67: *The temper tick is shown by a short, straight initial stroke.*

STEP ONE: *AN EXERCISE TO DECREASE TEMPER*

Write: **"forgiveness and humor will bend my temper"** five times per day for thirty days. Concentrate on bending each initial stroke into a "good humor flourish". Avoid making any short, straight "temper ticks."

Write out your first day's exercise here. For the next month write your exercises in a notebook acquired for this use alone. After one month, check back here and evaluate your progress.

_____

_____

_____

_____

_____

forgiveness and "humor" will bend my temper

This is an exercise to help you decrease your temper. As you **bend** each initial stroke in this exercise, consciously remind yourself that you are becoming less angry and your temper is diminishing with each stroke. *Beyond this exercise, consciously make these adjustments whenever your write.*

STEP TWO: *ACQUIRE GOOD SELF-CONTROL*

After a month of the above practice, you should begin an exercise to develop a POWER TRAIT that helps to counterbalance this RED FLAG. If your handwriting does not show ***GOOD SELF-CONTROL,*** look up the exercise for developing this trait. Eliminating a RED FLAG is best accomplished in a two-step program: 1) eradicating the negative stroke; and 2) developing a POWER TRAIT to fill a deficit that allowed the negative trait to form.

6. SELF CASTIGATION

God defend me from myself.

Montaigne

Self-castigation causes a person to feel unworthy of happiness or success. On one hand, the trait shows a bid for attention; on the other, it disables its possessor with self-provoked negative actions against himself.

Self-castigation is a vicious circle. When you blame yourself for something, others join all too willingly. Then, when you witness all these others pointing fingers, you become even more convinced of your own guilt.

This self-destructive trait is an unconscious attempt to absolve feelings of guilt, often about imagined wrongdoings. By indicting, trying and convicting yourself, you hope to earn some kind of clemency or forgiveness from the court; unfortunately, you have the least forgiving judge on the bench: yourself. Blaming yourself may be blaming the innocent.

Self castigation is a coin with two sides: **self-blame and self-punishment.** The punishment is seldom physical but may involve censuring yourself before others, depriving yourself of certain pleasures, even subjecting yourself to humiliation. To achieve gratification from this sort of self-punishment is unhealthy and unrealistic, often betraying insecurity. It is revealed by a final stroke that swings upward and backward over the preceding letters.

Fig. 68: *Self-castigation is revealed by final strokes that slash backward over the preceding letter.*

STEP ONE: *AN EXERCISE TO DECREASE SELF-CASTIGATION*

Write: **"stop trying to inflict self-hurt"** five times per day for thirty days. Concentrate on stopping each final stroke before it can arch back over preceding letters. You may want to practice making each final stroke curving gently upward at the end and stretching out to the right. If the straight portion of this stroke is as long as the preceding letter is wide, you have turned self-castigation into GENEROSITY, which may be applied to yourself as well.

Write out your first day's exercise here. For the next month write your exercises in a notebook acquired for this use alone. After one month, check back here and evaluate your progress.

_____

_____

_____

_____

This is an exercise to help you decrease your self-castigation. As you eliminate the back-slash final stroked in this exercise, consciously remind yourself that with each stroke you are becoming less inclined to blame and punish yourself. *Beyond this exercise, consciously make these adjustments whenever your write.*

STEP TWO: *ACQUIRE GOOD CONFIDENCE*

After a month of the above practice, you should begin an exercise to develop a POWER TRAIT that helps to counterbalance this RED FLAG. If your handwriting does not show **GOOD CONFIDENCE,** look up the exercise for developing this trait. Eliminating a RED FLAG is best accomplished in a two-step program: 1) eradicating the negative stroke; and 2) developing a POWER TRAIT to fill a deficit that allowed the negative trait to form.

7. JEALOUSY

Jealousy is one of the most destructive of all human emotion.

Eillism Todd

Jealousy is a desire to be the best and first in all areas of life, which of course is not possible. Being uncertain of yourself and your status in any given situation will bring jealousy out. Like a fever, jealousy often causes us to see things that are not really there, hallucinations that are mistaken for truth.

Jealousy is a fear of not being loved, a feeling of being inadequate, an anger at being bested. Because it is so complex a trait, it is not easily diminished. In handwriting it is revealed by tiny loops in the initial strokes that are flat on the bottom.

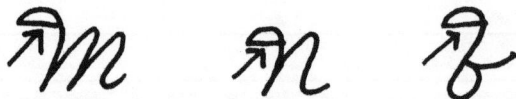

Fig 69: *Jealousy is shown by tiny flat loops in the initial strokes.*

STEP ONE: *AN EXERCISE TO DECREASE JEALOUSY*

Write: **"my main need is to nip jealousy"** five times per day for thirty days. Concentrate on eliminating the jealousy loops or turning them into "good humor flourishes" (see GOOD HUMOR exercise.)

Write out your first day's exercise here. For the next month write your exercises in a notebook acquired for this use alone. After one month, check back here and evaluate your progress.

This is an exercise to help you diminish your jealousy. As you eliminate all jealousy loops in this exercise, consciously remind yourself that you are becoming less jealous with each stroke. *Beyond this exercise, consciously make these adjustments whenever you write.*

STEP TWO: *ACQUIRE GREATER SELF-RELIANCE*

After a month of the above practice you should begin an exercise to develop a POWER TRAIT that helps to counterbalance this RED FLAG. If your handwriting does not show **SELF-RELIANCE,** look up the exercise for developing this trait. Eliminating a RED FLAG is best accomplished in a two-step program: 1) eradicating the negative stroke; and 2) developing a POWER TRAIT to fill a deficit that allowed the negative trait to form.

8. TOO MUCH CAUTION

Know, one false step is ne'er retrieved,
And be with caution bold.

Thomas Gray

Yes, the world can be a dangerous place to live. Those of us who are parents know that only too well; we've spent years teaching our children to be careful. **Caution is wisdom, we have told them. But a life that is lived with too much caution becomes a narrow, frightened life. The overly cautious person who cannot take chances or risk failure also will never succeed at great things.**

In social situations the overly cautious individual holds back, avoiding interaction with others for fear of judgment. Most often, however, this caution is unnecessary. Rarely do we find ourself in social situations as dangerous as that! Moderate and prudent caution is sufficient to avoid mistakes in our choices of social companions.

An entrepreneur who throws caution to the winds and succeeds is considered brilliant. If he fails, of course, he is a fool. No wonder so many who strive for great things have moments of doubt.

No one ever achieved anything great without some risk. Too much caution will insure that nothing is ventured; surely, then, nothing will be gained. **Learning to balance caution and risk is one of the first steps toward success.**

Caution is shown by **long,** straight final strokes or dashes at the end of letters or sentences. If this stroke is found frequently, it indicates too much caution.

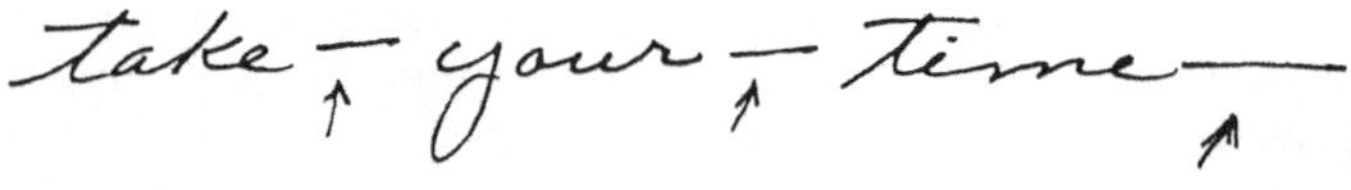

Fig. 70: Caution is revealed by long, straight final strokes or dashes at the end of letters or sentences.

STEP ONE: AN EXERCISE TO DIMINISH CAUTION

Write: **"one - two three I'm free"** five times per day for thirty days. Concentrate on eliminating **all but one** of the long dashes indicated above.

Write out your first day's exercise here. For the next month write your exercises in a notebook acquired for this use alone. After one month, check back here and evaluate your progress.

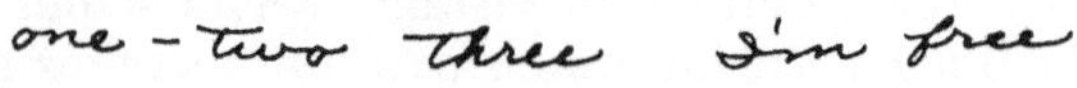

_____

_____

_____

_____

_____

This is an exercise to help you diminish your caution. As you eliminate some of the long dashes between letters and at the end of sentences, consciously remind yourself that you are becoming less **excessively** cautious with each stroke. _Beyond this exercise, consciously make these adjustments whenever you write._

STEP TWO: ACQUIRE GREATER INITIATIVE

After a month of the above practice you should begin an exercise to develop a POWER TRAIT that helps to counterbalance this RED FLAG. If your handwriting does not show **INITIATIVE**, look up the exercise for developing this trait. Eliminating a RED FLAG is best accomplished in a two-step program: 1) eradicating the negative stroke; and 2) developing a POWER TRAIT to fill a deficit that allowed the negative trait to form.

9. DESIRE FOR ATTENTION

Attention must be paid!
Arthur Miller
(Death of a Salesman)

Of course we all want attention from time to time. In this context it is a way of saying, "Hey, I'm unique and I deserve some attention. Listen to my ideas and don't treat me like others." Which is fine. **This trait becomes a RED FLAG, however, when it goes beyond the norm and becomes a desperate wish for attention deserved or not.**

The trait is revealed in handwriting by final strokes that push out to the right then up. It *starts* to go back to the left and then stops. It is not like self castigation which goes farther to the left.

Fig 71: Notice how the final strokes push out, then up, then it starts to go to the left but stops. This indicates desire for attention.

AN EXERCISE TO DECREASE THE DESIRE FOR ATTENTION

Write: **"I don't need this much attention"** five times per day for thirty days. Concentrate on not making the "desire for attention" final stroke. Instead, make each final stroke a gentle curve up, but do not start turning to the left.

Write out your first day's exercise here. For the next month write your exercises in a notebook acquired for this use alone. After one month, check back here and evaluate your progress.

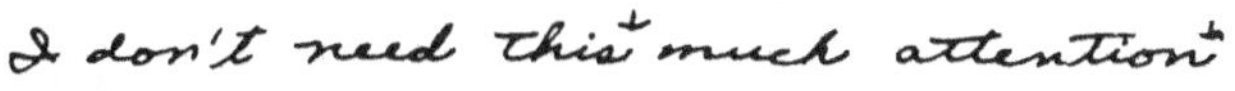

_____

_____

_____

_____

_____

I don't need this much attention

This is an exercise to help you decrease your desire for attention. As you adjust your final strokes in this exercise, consciously remind yourself that you are losing some of your desire for attention with each stroke. *Beyond this exercise, consciously make these adjustments whenever you write.*

STEP TWO: *ACQUIRE GREATER SELF-RELIANCE*

After a month of the above practice you should begin an exercise to develop a POWER TRAIT that helps to counterbalance this RED FLAG. If your handwriting does not show **SELF-RELIANCE,** look up the exercise for developing this trait. Eliminating a RED FLAG is best accomplished in a two-step program: 1) eradicating the negative stroke; and 2) developing a POWER TRAIT to fill a deficit that allowed the negative trait to form.

10. OVERLY STUBBORN

Those who never retract their opinions love themselves
more than they love truth.

Joseph Joubert

The "t's" tell us much about the personality. The tent-like "t", for example, indicates stubbornness. I like to tell people, **"It shows that you can't be easily convinced to change your mind."** This makes stubbornness sound more acceptable. You see, trying to convince a stubborn person to change butts heads directly against stubbornness itself. "Refusal to yield" perhaps is a better description of this trait.

Stubborn people usually write with heavy strokes. This indicates that they are a bit prejudiced, indicating that emotions are very strong about many issues.

Stubbornness seems to be a negative trait, but if you are stubborn in favor of your work, it could be beneficial. So stubbornness (refusal to yield) can be a good quality, too. **It is a matter of judgment.** How far has the stubbornness gone? **Too much stubbornness can be a defense mechanism in people who are afraid of admitting they don't know all the answers.** But being hard to convince can be a asset if you have high values and ideals.

This RED FLAG should be addressed **only if it is in the majority** of your writing, revealing an excessive amount of stubbornness. If the stroke occurs only occasionally, it indicates the potential for this trait.

Fig. 72: Stubbornness is shown by the tent-like formation of the downstroke in the "t" and the "d".

STEP ONE: *AN EXERCISE TO DECREASE STUBBORNNESS*
Write: **"stubbornness coded in letters t and d"** five times per day for thirty days. Concentrate on avoiding the "tent" formations shown above in each "d" and "t" stem.

Write out your first day's exercise here. For the next month write your exercises in a notebook acquired for this use alone. After one month, check back here and evaluate your progress.

_____

_____

_____

_____

_____

This is an exercise to help you decrease your stubbornness. As you avoid the tent shapes in this exercise, consciously remind yourself that you are becoming less stubborn with each stroke. *Beyond this exercise, consciously make these adjustments whenever you write.*

STEP TWO: *ACQUIRE GREATER BROADMINDEDNESS*
After a month of the above practice you should begin an exercise to develop a POWER TRAIT that helps to counterbalance this RED FLAG. If your handwriting does not show **BROADMINDEDNESS,** look up the exercise for developing this trait. Eliminating a RED FLAG is best accomplished in a two-step program: 1) eradicating the negative stroke; and 2) developing a POWER TRAIT to fill a deficit that allowed the negative trait to form.

11. SUPERFICIAL THINKING

Now mirth can into folly glide,
And folly into sin!

Sir Walter Scott

Loose, sloppy, or soft strokes in handwriting indicate superficial thought. This "softness" is a graphic representation of the "softness of thinking" in the writer.

A person who is guilty of superficial thinking looks only on the surface of matters, resulting in incomplete knowledge of things

which can be dangerous. Such a person is content with learning the obvious and reluctant to dig deeper.

If loose, unformed writing occurs only occasionally in your handwriting, as in a doctor's prescription, there is usually a reason. Often doctors and business executives do not want their handwriting copied so they write in a deliberately loose style that is hard to replicate. Other busy people really do not want to take time to communicate in handwriting, requiring a secretary to decipher and disseminate their messages. (I must confess that I often write in this way because of my busy schedule, preferring oral communication to written.) **If you occasionally write in this way, ask yourself why?**

If most or all of your handwriting shows this trait, then superficial thinking has become a dominant trait and the following exercises will be of help.

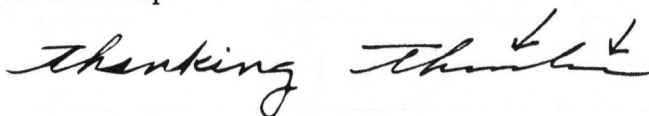

Fig. 73: Superficial thinking is shown by loose, sloppy, soft strokes, usually in "b", "c", "h", "k", "p", "m", and "n".

STEP ONE: *AN EXERCISE TO DECREASE SUPERFICIAL THINKING*

Write: *"thinking in depth"* five times per day for thirty days. Concentrate on making each stroke and letter well-formed with no looseness or softness in structure.

Write out your first day's exercise here. For the next month write your exercises in a notebook acquired for this use alone. After one month, check back here and evaluate your progress.

_____

_____

_____

_____

_____

This is an exercise to help you decrease superficial thought. As you make well-formed strokes in this exercise, consciously remind yourself that you are starting to think more deeply about everything with each stroke. *Beyond this exercise, consciously make these adjustments whenever you write.*

STEP TWO: DEVELOP YOUR DOMINANT THINKING PROCESS

After a month of the above practice you should begin an exercise to develop a POWER TRAIT that helps to counterbalance this RED FLAG. Go back to your INSIGHT PERSONALITY PROFILE and discover which of the five thinking processes is dominant in your writing. Then turn to the following **"Thinking Processes and Graphotherapy Exercises"** section to find the exercise that will help you develop your dominant thinking process. Eliminating a RED FLAG is best accomplished in a two-step program: 1) eradicating the negative stroke; and 2) developing a POWER TRAIT to fill a deficit that allowed the negative trait to form.

12. SHALLOW THINKING

Evidence of this trait is found in a bowl-shaped "t" crossing. If your handwriting reveals a frequent display of this stroke, **it means you are not using your intellectual gifts, preferring instead to avoid profound thoughts or questions and to ignore your mind's potential. It is a kind of mental complacency.**

Do not mistake this for a sign of inferior intelligence. It is not an IQ rating, but rather an indication that you are not trying, perhaps because you do not care to think more deeply or do not believe you can. The bowl-shaped stroke is usually caused by a lack of self-reliance or self-confidence, a failure to believe in yourself and your mental abilities. And yet you have chosen to read this book. You have chosen to improve yourself. By comparison, the next step is quite simple: give the following exercises a chance.

Fig. 74: Shallow thinking is revealed by bowl-shaped "t" crossings.

STEP ONE: *AN EXERCISE TO*
DECREASE SHALLOW THINKING

Write; **"today I test my true intelligence"** five times per day for thirty days. Concentrate on making each "t" crossing straight and one step higher on the stem than you ordinarily make it. This will also improve your SELF-CONFIDENCE as you eliminate the dish-shaped shallow thinking stroke.

Write out your first day's exercise here. For the next month write your exercises in a notebook acquired for this use alone. After one month, check back here and evaluate your progress.

Today I test my true intelligence

This is an exercise to help you decrease your shallow thinking. As you make a straight "t" crossings in this exercise. Consciously remind yourself that you are starting to utilize more of your intelligence with each stroke. _Beyond this exercise, consciously make these adjustments whenever you write._

STEP TWO: _DEVELOP YOUR DOMINANT THINKING_

After a month of the above practice you should begin an exercise to develop a POWER TRAIT that helps to counterbalance this RED FLAG. Go back to your INSIGHT PERSONALITY PROFILE and discover which of the five thinking processes is dominant in your writing. Then turn to the following **_"Thinking Processes and Graphotherapy Exercises"_** section to find the exercise that will help you develop your dominant thinking process. Eliminating a RED FLAG is best accomplished in a two-step program: 1) eradicating the negative stroke; and 2) developing a POWER TRAIT to fill a deficit that allowed the negative trait to form.

13. REPRESSION

Repression differs from suppression in nature and effect, but both are defensive traits. Repression is an automatic and un-conscious act of burying memories, usually unpleasant ones, that then become forgotten — unavailable to the conscious mind — but continue subconsciously to affect behavior. It is like having a disease but not knowing about it. The disease can gnaw away at our health, but we don't know it's there until too late.

Suppression, on the other hand, is a _conscious_ and often temporary effort to tuck away unpleasant memories, sometimes just so we can get on with other business. Suppression can become repression if feelings, thoughts and memories are constantly buried and not brought back to the conscious level to be dealt with at the appropriate time.

To spot these traits in handwriting, look for an upward retracing of the downstroke in such letters as "h", "m", "n", and "r". An occasional retracing indicates suppression, which is sometimes necessary to get through the day. A frequent retracing, however, reveals repression and should be corrected through the following exercises.

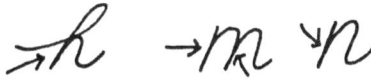

Fig. 75: Repression is shown by frequent upward retracing of downstrokes in the letters "h", "m", "n", and "r".

STEP ONE: *AN EXERCISE TO DECREASE REPRESSION*

Write: **"humans are forever hiding pain"** five times per day for thirty days. Concentrate on avoiding any retracing in the letters "h", "m", "n", and "r". Open up a little space between the downstroke in these letters and the following upstroke.

Write out your first day's exercise here. For the next month write your exercises in a notebook acquired for this use alone. After one month, check back here and evaluate your progress.

_____

_____

_____

_____

_____

This is an exercise to help you decrease your repression. As you avoid retracing of strokes in this exercise, consciously remind yourself that you are releasing old pain and becoming less repressed with each stroke. *Beyond this exercise, consciously make these adjustments whenever you write.*

STEP TWO: *ACQUIRE GREATER BROADMINDEDNESS*

After a month of the above practice you should begin an exercise to develop a POWER TRAIT that helps to counterbalance this RED FLAG. If your handwriting does not show **BROADMINDEDNESS**, look up the exercise for developing this trait. Eliminating a RED

FLAG is best accomplished in a two-step program: 1) eradicating the negative stroke; and 2) developing a POWER TRAIT to fill a deficit that allowed the negative trait to form.

14. CONFUSION

Swift as a shadow, short as any dream,
So quick bright things come to confusion...

Shakespeare

Let's face it, life is complicated. In the course of living, the mind can sometimes become overwhelmed with so many messages, so much information, so little time to process it all.

Confusion sets in when thinking becomes too busy. The result is a lack of priorities and planning, frequent mix-ups, and disorganized actions. Interestingly, people who are highly creative and enterprising frequently show this trait in their handwriting. Apparently, there is so much going on in their minds that confusion becomes the first step of a creative process: the old axiom of making order out of chaos. The risk, of course, is that the mind may spend a lot of time whirring away to find an exit and never work its way out of this confusion.

Confusion is best avoided. It saps time and energy. It sends us down too many fruitless paths. It can create chaos in our relationships and throughout the rest of our lives.

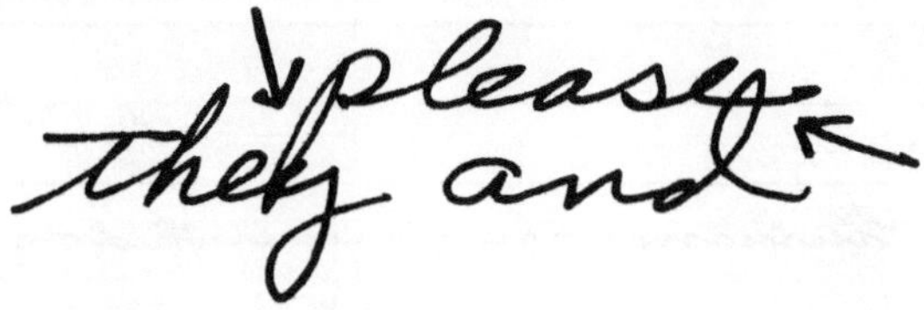

Fig 76: *Upstrokes that run into the line above, or downstrokes that overlap the line below, indicate confusion.*

STEP ONE: *AN EXERCISE TO DECREASE CONFUSION*

Write: **"thinking clearly and orderly"** five times per day for thirty days. Concentrate on avoiding any overlap of strokes from one line to the other. Put as much space between written lines as necessary, skipping lines if you have to.

Write out your first day's exercise here. For the next month write your exercises in a notebook acquired for this use alone. After one month, check back here and evaluate your progress.

Thinking clearly and orderly
Thinking clearly and orderly

This is an exercise to help you decrease your confusion. As you eliminate the overlapping strokes in this exercise, consciously remind yourself that you are becoming less confused and thinking more clearly and orderly with each stroke. *Beyond this exercise, consciously make these adjustments whenever you write.*

STEP TWO: *ACQUIRE ORGANIZATIONAL ABILITY*

After a month of the above practice you should begin an exercise to develop a POWER TRAIT that helps to counterbalance this RED FLAG. If your handwriting does not show **ORGANIZATIONAL ABILITY,** look up the exercise for developing this trait. Eliminating a RED FLAG is best accomplished in a two-step program: 1) eradicating the negative stroke; and 2) developing a POWER TRAIT to fill a deficit that allowed the negative trait to form.

15. DOMINEERING

No two... can be half an hour together but one will
acquire an evident superiority over the other.

Samuel Johnson

The domineering personality influences others by pressure and force of will. The form may be subtle yet direct, or may involve an emotional outburst. If you are domineering, you often resort to manipulation of many kinds in causing others to yield to your plan or will. Your actions show a disdain for other people and frequently you can be a nag. In handwriting, look for a "t" crossing that slants down to the right and tapers to a point.

This tiresome trait is an attempt to make up for other power traits that would enable mature action and generate mutual respect. As a result, the domineering person resorts to immature, adaptive habits. These may succeed in influencing people in the short run, but over time the domineering person loses friends and power.

Fig. 77: A domineering personality is shown by a "t" crossing that slants down to the right and tapers to a point.

STEP ONE: *AN EXERCISE TO DECREASE A DOMINEERING NATURE*

Write: **"try to let others live their lives"** five times per day for thirty days. Concentrate on making each "t" crossing straight and absolutely horizontal, crossing through the stem completely.

Write out your first day's exercise here. For the next month write your exercises in a notebook acquired for this use alone. After one month, check back here and evaluate your progress.

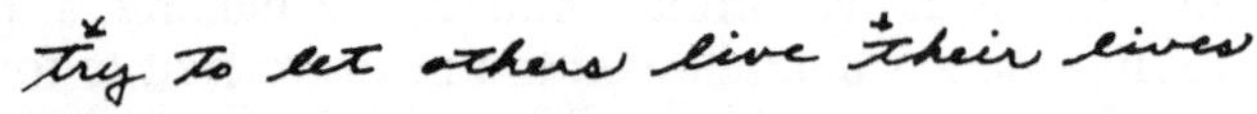

_____

_____

_____

_____

_____

try to let others live their lives

This is an exercise to help you decrease your domineering nature. As you make straight, horizontal "t" crossings in this exercise, consciously remind yourself that you are becoming less sensitive about yourself with each stroke. *Beyond this exercise, consciously make these adjustments whenever you write.*

STEP TWO: *ACQUIRE GREATER BROADMINDEDNESS*

After a month of the above practice you should begin an exercise to develop a POWER TRAIT that helps to counterbalance this RED FLAG. If your handwriting does not show **BROADMINDEDNESS,** look up the exercise for developing this trait. Eliminating a RED FLAG is best accomplished in a two-step program: 1) eradicating the negative stroke; and 2) developing a POWER TRAIT to fill a deficit that allowed the negative trait to form.

THE THINKING PROCESSES AND GRAPHOTHERAPY EXERCISES

1. ANALYTICAL THINKING

A "v" shape that occurs in certain middle zone letters is evidence of an analytical mind. This is an extremely positive trait for it enhances and strengthens all other mental processes that are present.

This "v" shape can be found between the two humps of the "m" and between the downstroke and hump of the "n". Look for it also in the "r", formed by the final upstroke, and at the bottom of the "w".

This trait is found in middle zone letters, indicating that the analytical thinking process involves continually analyzing facts to arrive at daily decisions. A person who thinks in this fashion is able to deal with an abundance of information without confusion and is able to draw conclusions when others cannot.

The analytical thinking process may be thought of as a powerful tool.

Fig. 78: Analytical thinking is shown by "v" shapes that occur in the "m", "n", "r", and "w".

AN EXERCISE FOR ANALYTICAL THINKING

Write: **"my writing will get sharper"** five times per day for thirty days. Concentrate on making the sharp, pointed "v" shapes in the letters "m", "n", "r", and "w" as illustrated above.

Write out your first day's exercise here. For the next month write your exercises in a notebook acquired for this use alone. After one month, check back here and evaluate your progress.

_____

_____

_____

_____

_____

my writing will get sharpere

This is an exercise to help you acquire or sharpen your analytical mind. As you make the sharp "v" shapes in this exercise, consciously remind yourself that you are gaining analytical ability with each stroke. *Beyond this exercise, consciously make these adjustments whenever you write.*

2. EXPLORATORY THINKING

Of all the thinking processes, **this is the most adventuresome.** A person who is exploratory in thinking essentially is unafraid to chart new courses and kick over new stones. **Such a mind moves out into the unknown with few preconceptions, eager for discovery.**

When encountering a problem, this person does not rely merely on the facts as they are known to fashion a solution, but rather sets out to find *missing* information, a *different* approach, an *unknown* relationship between the pieces of the puzzle. **Mentally, this person is a discoverer, relishing the new find almost as much as its contribution to a larger whole. Such an intensely curious person never mentally drills a "dry hole" deeper into the ground, preferring instead to drill many holes and cover more ground.**

On a social plane, this person can be exciting and invigorating to be with; the **curious mind** has also a curiously stimulating effect on others.

This trait shows up in handwriting as sharp "mountain peaks", almost as if the "explorer" needed them to conquer. These inverted "v" shapes often appear in the letters "h", "m", "n" "p", "w", and sometimes at the top of the "l" loop (which indicates exploratory thinking in the philosophical or abstract area.)

Fig., 79: *Exploratory thinking shows as inverted "v's" - or "mountain tops" in these letters.*

AN EXERCISE FOR EXPLORATORY THINKING

Write: **explore the world of the mind"** five times per day for thirty days. Concentrate on making the sharp "inverted v" shapes as shown in the examples above.

Write out your first day's exercise here. For the next month write your exercises in a notebook acquired for this use alone. After one month, check back here and evaluate your progress.

This is an exercise to help you acquire or sharpen your exploratory thinking. As you make the "inverted v's" in this exercise, consciously remind yourself that you are gaining a more curious and exploratory nature with each stroke. *Beyond this exercise, consciously make these pointed "mountain tops" whenever you write.*

3. KEEN COMPREHENSION

What a man doesn't understand,
He doesn't have.

Goethe

Keen comprehension is the ability to understand ideas and situations *quickly*. **The word "comprehension" literally means to "grasp mentally."** The keenly comprehensive mind "understands" concepts and processes almost before they have been revealed. Sometimes understanding comes so quickly it almost makes one want to cry out, "Eureka!" (Occasionally this leads to frustration, when understanding comes well before the end of a painfully long explanation.)

The "World's Best Lovers" are always those who are most responsive to their partners, understanding of their needs. Keen comprehension allows a lover to pick up and understand even the tiniest signals from a partner. This creates an almost psychic sense of "knowing" what the other person wants.

Can you walk into a party and size up the room at a glance? With a party of good friends, it's a cinch. You know their moods and behaviors so well, if something is amiss you can catch it right off. But if you have a keenly comprehensive mind, you can catch the same subtle signals in a roomful of strangers. You can understand the social pecking order almost immediately and know who is angry or standoffish. You'd be less likely to make the kind of social faux pas we all fear.

Keen comprehension also makes you a good conversationalist. You are seldom at a loss for words because you quickly see to the heart of a conversation and join in appropriately. You immediately understand what others are saying, or trying to say, and sometimes you can even help them explain their points.

The ability to discover quickly the heart of a problem makes this trait almost indispensable for the person in business, the artist, the journalist... the Mom! Success is usually the culmination of a long series of problems solved in a timely fashion. If you can grasp things quickly, you can achieve your goals that much sooner. The keenly comprehensive mind wastes no time on the road to success.

As you've probably guessed, KEEN COMPREHENSION and ATTENTION TO DETAILS go hand in hand. They enhance each other. "Details" are the input to the computer in your head; "comprehension" is knowing what to do with them.

Fig. 80: Keen comprehension is shown by sharp, "needlepoint" strokes.

AN EXERCISE TO INCREASE COMPREHENSION

Write: **"my writing shows a comprehending mind"** five times per day for thirty days. Work hard on creating or developing the sharp "needlepoint" strokes on the tops of the letters "h", "m", "n", "r" and "w".

Write out your first day's exercise here. For the next month write your exercises in a notebook acquired for this use alone. After one month, check back here and evaluate your progress.

_____

_____

_____

_____

my writing shows a comprehending mind

This is an exercise to help you increase your comprehension. As you sharpen your "needlepoint" strokes in this exercise, consciously remind yourself that you are developing your powers of comprehension with each stroke. *Beyond this exercise, consciously adjust your strokes in these middle zone letters each time you write.*

4. LOGICAL THINKING

"Contrariwise," continued Tweedledee,
"If it was so, it might be;
and if it were so, it would be.
But it isn't, so it ain't
That's logic."

Lewis Carroll

A logical thinker considers ideas in his mind before he expresses them. Such a person thinks thoroughly and accurately. He follows directions carefully and has the ability to do so.. Good, sound judgments come from logical thinking, sometimes called "cumulative" thinking because it requires the accumulation of information to provide the basis for orderly judgment.

People who think in a logical way fall in love with their minds first; the heart follows after much consideration. The brain may think lightening-fast but decisions are made carefully. In handwriting, logical thinking is shown by the same strokes that reveal manual dexterity (flat-top "r's" and rounded tops on "m's" and "n's".)

$$\overset{\downarrow}{\smallsmile} \quad \overset{\downarrow}{\mathcal{m}} \quad \mathcal{n}$$

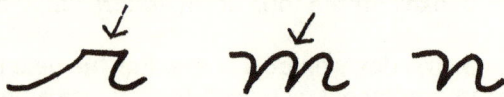

Fig. 81: Logical thinking is revealed by flat-topped "r's" and rounded "m's" and "n's".

AN EXERCISE FOR LOGICAL THINKING

Write: **"my thinking is orderly"** five times per day for thirty days. Concentrate on making each "r" with a flat top and each "m" and "n" rounded on each hump.

Write out your first day's exercise here. For the next month write your exercises in a notebook acquired for this use alone. After one month, check back here and evaluate your progress.

_____

_____

_____

_____

my thinking is orderly

This is an exercise to help you improve or acquire logical thinking. As you make round "m's" and "n's", and flat-topped "r's" in this exercise, consciously remind yourself that your thinking is becoming more logical and orderly with each stroke. *Beyond this exercise, consciously adjust these middle zone letters whenever you write.*

5. INTUITIVE THINKING

*... One in whom persuasion and belief
Had ripened into faith, and faith become
A passionate intuition.*

William Wordsworth

Intuitiveness gives its possessor insight into problems or relationships. It is an uncanny knowing of things not revealed by facts or other evidence. Intuition, once developed is a great aid to all other thinking processes. In handwriting, it is shown by a break between connecting letters in a word. It is almost as if the mind of the intuitive writer hesitates or perceives solutions without knowing how this knowledge is acquired.

Intuition gives people a "sixth sense" about the truthfulness of things, the genuine quality of a person, even the likelihood of success of a particular endeavor. It is a clue, a revelation, an inkling that nudges the mind in one direction or the other. It brings to the surface a nearly psychic insight that makes use of all one's senses plus something quite undefinable, as if the mind has become a divining rod drawing all other faculties toward ultimate truth or solution.

in tui tive

Fig. 82: Intuitive thinking is shown by frequent breaks between letter structures.

AN EXERCISE FOR INTUITIVE THINKING

Write; **"my intuition is being developed"** five times per day for thirty days. Concentrate on making breaks between many of the letters in these words without resorting to printing.

Write out your first day's exercise here. For the next month write your exercises in a notebook acquired for this use alone. After one month, check back here and evaluate your progress.

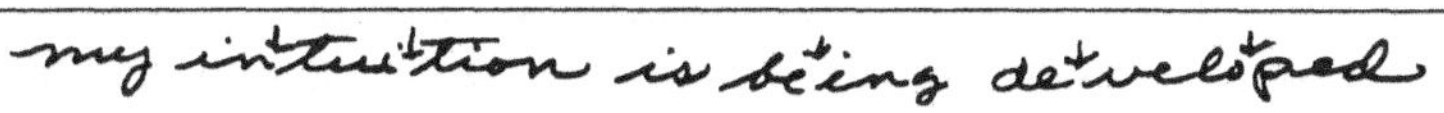

_____

_____

_____

_____

my intuition is being developed

This is an exercise to help you improve your intuitiveness. As you make breaks between the letters in this exercise, consciously remind yourself that you are becoming more intuitive with each stroke. *Beyond this exercise, consciously make breaks between letter structures whenever you write.*

POWER STROKES AND YOUR LIFE

Over the years, people have asked me many questions about which POWER TRAITS are desirable in certain areas of their lives. These questions always have seemed to fall within four broad areas of living: sex, social life, the arts, and business. Since I cannot respond to your specific questions in person, I've charted the POWER TRAITS and their importance to each of these four areas.

Opposite each POWER TRAIT, an "X" indicates a high level of importance to the checked category. While an argument can be made that POWER TRAITS left unchecked under the "SEX" category, for example, may also be important to that area of one's life, the designated traits are certainly important.

This chart offers an alternative plan for determining which traits you may wish to acquire or develop. From this chart choose the area of living you wish to develop more fully, then compare this category's designated POWER TRAITS with your own "chart of accounts" — the results of your INSIGHT PERSONALITY PROFILE. Determine which missing POWER TRAIT you want to develop first, then look up the appropriate exercise.

Remember, work on no more than one trait — one handwriting exercise — at a time, and give each exercise at least thirty days of concentration.

POWER TRAITS BY AREA OF LIVING

		SEX	SOCIAL	ART	BUSINESS
1	SELF-RELIANCE	XXX	XXX	XXX	XXX
2	GOOD GOALS	XXX	XXX	XXX	XXX
3	GOOD CONFIDENCE	XXX	XXX	XXX	XXX
4	ATTENTION TO DETAILS	XXX	XXX	XXX	XXX
5	KEEN COMPREHENSION		XXX		XXX
6	WILL POWER				XXX
7	ENTHUSIASM	XXX	XXX	XXX	XXX
8	INITIATIVE	XXX			XXX
9	ORGANIZING ABILITY				XXX
10	PHILOSOPHICAL IMAGIN	XXX	XXX	XXX	XXX
	MATERIAL IMAGINATION	XXX	XXX	XXX	XXX
11	DECISIVENESS				XXX
12	DETERMINATION				XXX
13	PERSISTENCE				XXX
14	DIPLOMACY	XXX	XXX		XXX
15	EXPLORATORY THINKING			XXX	
16	OPTIMISM		XXX		XXX
17	TALKATIVENESS		XXX		
18	SENSE OF HUMOR	XXX	XXX		
19	BROADMINDED	XXX	XXX		
20	LOYALTY	XXX		XXX	
21	MANUAL DEXTERITY	XXX		XXX	
22	GENEROSITY	XXX	XXX	XXX	XXX
23	GOOD SELF-CONTROL	XXX	XXX	XXX	
24	LOVES PHYS ACTIVITY	XXX	XXX	XXX	XXX
25	INTUITIVE THINKING	XXX	XXX	XXX	XXX
26	LOGICAL THINKING	XXX	XXX		
27	GOOD COLOR SENSE	XXX	XXX		XXX
28	INDEPENDENT THINKING			XXX	
29	LITERARY INCLINATION			XXX	
30	PURSUE ARTISTIC AREA			XXX	

QUESTIONS AND ANSWERS

After thousands of personal handwriting analyses and many hours of listener response on my radio program, I've heard just about every kind of question about this remarkable field of graphotherapy. Naturally, certain questions are asked over and over again. I've written the answers to these most-asked questions and put them here; perhaps your most unanswered questions are among them.

QUESTION: *Can you use a signature as a handwriting sample to determine a person's personality?*

ELAYNE: Signatures tell us a lot about the person who the writer would *like* to be. Many signatures are artificially concocted and practiced to project a desired effect. And usually a signature does not provide enough of a sample to make accurate judgments.

QUESTION: *Can't a person change his handwriting?*

ELAYNE: You can never change your handwriting completely. You can change certain strokes, as in the graphotherapy exercises included in this book, and this will produce a corollary change in the related personality trait. But as for forgers, no — there are always a few strokes that will betray him.

QUESTION: *Can you tell a person's age by handwriting analysis?*

ELAYNE: Not reliably. It is sometimes possible to tell a young writer, someone under the age of 11 or 12. Youngsters often have a slightly "elementary" style to their writing; they are not far enough away from the penmanship classes in school. Elderly people sometimes reveal their advanced age through a shaking or quavering in the strokes, but this same squiggliness can show up in the handwriting of someone who is ill.

QUESTION: *I am a right-hander, but I can write to make myself look like a left-hander. Would that change your analysis of my handwriting?*

ELAYNE: I'm not sure what you think a left-hander's writing looks like, but I'll bet you assume it shows a slant: backhand or "backslant." This is a common misconception. Left-handers do not always write with a backslant, and some right-handers do. Would your "change" in writing alter my analysis? No, the same basic strokes will occur in your handwriting regardless of how you think you are changing your writing.

QUESTION: *What does it tell you when a person prefers to print or print in capital letters rather than write?*

ELAYNE: It tells me the individual has a strong desire for simplicity and probably leans toward the artistic or creative side. Analysis of printing, by the way, follows the same rules as for script except, of course, there are no upper or lower loops to analyze.

QUESTION: *How about writing that shows both script and printing in the same sentence?*

ELAYNE: Once again, printing without being instructed to do so means the writer is creative. Printing is like drawing little pictures on canvas. A person who mixes script with printing in the same sentence is creative but probably in a hurry. The slower printing is abandoned from time to time in favor of a quicker cursive script.

QUESTION: *What does it mean when I write differently? The letters I write are not always consistent in shape.*

ELAYNE: It means you're individualistic. You don't want to go along with what you were taught. This may be positive sign in handwriting.

QUESTION: *What's the significance of a very light stroke in a letter, in fact one made so light it barely shows up?*

ELAYNE: It could be the writer is just in a hurry. A hurried writer sometimes uses abnormally light pressure. As a rule, however, the lightness or heaviness of a stroke indicates the relative forcefulness of the personality trait. If the light stroke in question happens to be a "t" crossing, for example, it means there is not much force behind that associated trait.

I'll give you an example: procrastination. If you make a "t" crossing in front of the "t" stem, failing to cross the stem, it reveals procrastination. If this "t" crossing is made very light, it means the procrastination has little force. The light touch, then minimizes the negativity of this potential RED FLAG.

QUESTION: Will my handwriting change depending on my mood?

ELAYNE: Yes, for example, when I write checks to pay bills my handwriting reveals the "temper tick." My anger at having to part with money shows in my handwriting at the time I am experiencing that emotion. Other strokes can be affected, too. Some days you may feel more withdrawn; on others you may be feeling deeply about things. These and other moods and emotions are reflected in your handwriting. When my son was in the Army I could tell from his letters when he was depressed and when he was "up." (He must have gotten tired of my questions, though; he started typing his letters.)

QUESTION: You mentioned depression. Is this shown in hand-writing? It does not show up in this book as a RED FLAG.

ELAYNE: Depression is not a primary trait; that is, it cannot be identified by a simple stroke. Depression is what we call an "evaluated" trait. A handwriting sample that shows very limited goals, self-castigation, and a general "dropping down" of letters in written words would be "evaluated" as depression. And there are other combinations of traits that can reveal this mood. The book you are reading, however, **deals only with primary traits** and so depression is not listed.

QUESTION: Does nervousness show up in handwriting?

ELAYNE: At times nervousness shows as a slight wavering throughout the handwriting sample.

QUESTION: Couldn't it be dangerous for parents who are not expert in handwriting analysis to start changing their children's handwriting strokes?

ELAYNE: Yes, I think so. Change must be approached in a structured way. I don't necessarily advocate *changing* the handwriting of children. Rather, **I suggest that parents use a basic knowledge of handwriting strokes to understand their children better.** What a marvelous tool for understanding!

Of course the handwriting of children can be changed. **My research has shown this.** But without a detailed, advanced knowledge of handwriting analysis and graphotherapy, a parent faces some peril in attempting to remodel his or her impressionable youngsters. In this area, a little knowledge certainly can be a dangerous thing.

QUESTION: *Can handwriting analysis tell if two people are compatible?*

ELAYNE: Yes, it's a great tool for people deciding to have a relationship. Unfortunately, most people in love don't heed the evidence of incompatibility. I recall one couple that came to me for a thorough compatibility analysis. My report showed several areas where there was a striking clash. They thanked me, said they could work those things out, and got married. Five years later they were divorced.

Handwriting analysis is not fortune telling. But it can show where problems in relationships may exist, and where future problems could arise. The couple above may have learned from the compatibility analysis and worked hard on resolving the issues (it would have taken *much* hard work in their case, however.) Graphotherapy may have helped to solve some of their tougher incompatibilities. But clearly the issues were not solved and the result was a divorce. I never tell people *not* to have a relationship. I only hope that the knowledge they gain from my work will help them have a *successful* relationship if they choose to pursue it.

Elayne V. Lindberg with Gary Lindberg

THE INDEX

Elayne's original acknowledgements are reprinted here in her memory and the memory of all those she acknowledged and have passed away.

ACKNOWLEDGEMENTS

There is hardly room in such a slender volume for the long list of friends and associates who aided me in the creation of this book, To all of you who I am not able to publicly acknowledge, please accept my sincere thank you for your time, expertise, guidance, ideas and wishes of success, There are a select few, however, who I must go on record for having acknowledged directly, because without them this book never would have been written and published.

First, my dear friend Steve Edelman of KSTP-TV, After an appearance on his television show four years ago, Steve urged me to take my research and write this book, The idea was born, and I give full credit to Steve for igniting the spark, Then, my sensitive, perceptive daughter Bonnie, also my business partner in several art galleries, who urged me to "Get started!" when the challenge suddenly seemed more than I could face; and who contributed immeasurably by writing the first outline of the material and introducing many of the structural ideas, Also my husband, who unfailingly supported me until the very end, helped literally with every aspect of the book (including ALL the illustrations), and helped organize a mammoth amount of research.

I must also acknowledge Dr. Stanley Shapiro, who gave me so much support over the years and whose wisdom and understanding of humankind is something to which I shall always aspire; Lil Peterson, my faithful assistant who diligently typed and retyped draft after draft of the manuscript; and Bill Mack, a generous and talented sculptor, who allowed me to use many of the signatures from his collection of famous people to illustrate this book.

Elayne V. Lindberg

ABOUT THE AUTHORS

Elayne Lindberg, MGA

Elayne was a Certified Graphoanalyst and pioneer in the field of questioned documents. For several decades she was an expert court witness working for the Minnesota Attorney General's office, numerous police departments, attorneys, corporations, medical professionals and individuals. She was a charter member of the World Association of Document Examiners, a member of the International Society of Graphoanalysis, and was a Certified Master Graphoanalyst. She spent seventeen years researching the specialty of graphotherapeutics.

Gary Lindberg

Elayne's son, Gary, is a filmmaker, author and publisher. He co-wrote and produced the Paramount film *That Was Then, This Is Now* starring Morgan Freeman and Emilio Estevez, as well as countless TV commercials, corporate films and special programs for cable TV. He is the author of four consecutive Amazon bestselling novels and founder of Calumet Editions, which publishes quality fiction and nonfiction books. He has won over one hundred national and international awards for his media work.

Gratitude for the Work of
Elayne Lindberg

"Mrs. Lindberg is an extremely sensitive and competent graphoanalyst. She has done handwriting analysis for some of my patients. I was impressed with the depth and accuracy of her reports, which gave me an early clue to potential problem areas. At other times, her analyses helped me to focus on areas which resulted in a breakthrough in the patients' resistance to progress.

I gave her a sample of my handwriting 19 years ago, before she knew me, and was surprised and somewhat embarrassed by the accuracy of her report.

Her current research expands the work of previous authors, specifically the concept of changing a particular writing stroke in order to modify the personality trait connected with it. It is an interesting concept, one which I believe merits investigation and embracing."

- Stanley W. Shapiro, M.D., Psychiatrist

"The learned skill of writing is as indelible as a fingrprint to a skilled graphologist. A skilled graphologist is, after all, looking at the representational system of someone who writes and represents the external/internal world subjectively. The handwriting is a product of every experience that has impacted the person in question.

If the development of muscles and neurological development are considered, the act of writing entails hours of practice with the sending of signals from the hand to the brain and back again. These loops of signals are imprinted on the brain in much the same way as crawling, walking and running.

Writing becomes identifiable in a clinical sense, and provides us with clues to personality disorders, and the sum total of our experiences. For those of us who make decisions abut the clinical attributes of personality, the additional information provided by unconcious clues make the task that much easier.

For these, and many more reasons, I am grateful to Elayne Lindberg for devoting endless hours of labor and interpretive skill to a greater understanding of the written handwriting strokes and what they mean."

—James Joseph Duffey, Ph.D., Psychotherapist